Time Management Mastery: Productivity & Goals

Gaurav Sanjiv Kalangan

Published by Gaurav Sanjiv Kalangan, 2024.

Also by Gaurav Sanjiv Kalangan

Learn Options Strategies Options Basics & Greeks For Stock Trading By Technical Analysis

Bitcoin, Altcoins & ICOs Learn the Basics of Digital Coins from Zero

Time Management This Is How I Work 300 Percent Faster

How To Build And Implement A Winning Pricing Strategy

Networking For Introverts: Gracefully Exiting A Conversation

Accounting 101: Learn Cost Accounting From A To Z

Growth Marketing: Strategy & Execution Bootcamp For Startups

Develop The Mental Strength Of A Warrior For Success In Life

Time Management Mastery: Productivity & Goals

Table of Contents

Copyright

Published by Gaurav Sanjiv Kalangan

Copyright © 2024 Gaurav Sanjiv Kalangan

All rights reserved.

Distributed by Gaurav Sanjiv Kalangan

Time Management Mastery: Productivity & Goals

Design and composition by Gaurav Sanjiv Kalangan Cover design by Gaurav Sanjiv Kalangan For permission credits.

To offset the number of trees consumed in the printing of our books, Gaurav Sanjiv Kalangan donates a portion of the proceeds from each printing to the Arbor Day Foundation. Gaurav Sanjiv Kalangan has replaced over 50 trees since 2022.

First Edition

I dedicate this to the dreamers, healers, and givers who deliver value through art and invention, expression, and creation. With all my love.

About

Effective time management is the secret to enjoying life and having a successful career. It dictates how much stress will affect you, how often you see your family, how good you are at your job and even how happy you will be throughout your life. However, it's not something that's easy to get right. This Book will teach you practical daily habits to help you master productivity and get your work life balance back on track.

Do you feel like you've always got a never-ending list of jobs to be done? That you don't even know where to start? Do you often wake up feeling stressed and anxious? Are you struggling to find the time to do the things that you really enjoy? This Book will help you work out what's fundamentally important to you and help you to focus on it better, and do more of it. Whether you want to excel in your career or to live a happier, more-fulfilled personal life, this Book will arm you with a robust skill set that will change your life.

Every day when you get up, you have a choice. How are you going to spend your time that day? Will you climb into bed exhausted and unhappy or will you fall asleep with a smile on your face knowing that you're one step closer to achieving your goals? Your life is only time and how you use your time not only has a huge effect on how much you achieve during your life, but also how much you enjoy yourself during your life. Many of us will happily waste hours on stuff that's not important at all. But the idea of allocating our time in the same way that we would budget or allocate our money can be quite a difficult concept to put in place.

First we'll look at the really big picture of how you decide what's most important to you in your life. We'll talk about goal setting, work life balance and some of the skills of effective time management, like negotiating and delegation. Then we'll funnel down into the nitty gritty details like what you should have on your desk, what your email footer should say and how these can help you master productivity.

By the time you finish this Book, you will have a set of skills that will allow you to banish procrastination and start living a productive, efficient and happier life. From learning when to say no, to setting aside time for yourself every day, this Book will motivate you to take control of your life and achieve your goals.

Stop wasting your time and start living a more productive, happier life today!

Welcome

Hi there, and welcome to my Book on Time and Productivity Management. I'm delighted to have you here. And my hope is that this Book will argue with the philosophy, knowledge and tools to take back your time. If the ever elusive phenomenon and commodity, that is time as a 40 new sightings that are far and few in between, then you are exactly where you need to be. This Book was put together with the single purpose of acting as an enabler for people from any and all walks of life to take back their time, increase their productivity, and to effectively get it all done. The Book is a combination of philosophical ideals, tried and tested methodologies, research examples and exercises that will assist you in really grasping the value of the seemingly simple techniques that will drastically improve the use of your time.

Before we start, I want to share with you what I believe to be the keys to self-improvement and there are two personality aspects that you have already demonstrated just by being where you are now and listening to me talk. Number one is the aspiration to improve and to obtain more out of your life. You would not be here if you didn't want to improve yourself and get closer to your goals. And number two is the wisdom to know that you need not try and effect these changes you desire without help and tools, which is the second reason why you're here. You want to arm yourself with the tools you need to take that next step and improve upon your boshoff. These are two very important qualities in life and in the pursuit of improvement.

And I want to commend you for demonstrating them both here. You are already ready to make the change you want and deserve all you need to do now. So give me a few hours of your time to arm you with the tools you need to do so. We are going to start off discussing the philosophical truth about time and its real value, and not in a boring way. The idea is to really imprint the actual value of time in your thoughts so that we can then build upon that with knowledge and practical actions that you learn here to really scratch the surface and get your hands on that value. From there, we will cover the basics of time wasters. Then we will take a look at the individual. In other words, you and how your uniqueness impacts your time management and your ability to use your time effectively.

With all the background information in place, we will then tackle the various productivity techniques you can use to create your own productivity system. In my experience, real learning is a combination of the acquisition of knowledge and the implementation of techniques. It is for this reason that the Book not only teaches you what you need to know, but also challenges you to practice what you've learned in a structured and systematic manner. I urge you now to please commit to actually doing each of the exercises and challenges as thoroughly as you possibly can, because without actual practice, you will not be able to get the full benefit out of this Book.

What to Expect From the Book

The structure of this Book was designed to create an easy to navigate outline with a firm focus on efficiency and optimal use of time. Each chapter was carefully laid out to facilitate an almost narrative development of the key concepts and actions, thus ensuring that the primary message of the subchapter chapters is conveyed as strongly as possible. In addition, the chapters have been kept brief and to the point with clearly identifiable names. All of this was done to create an easily referenced Oppel guide ideal for refreshing key concepts at later stages. The first chapter of the Book serves as introduction and provides all the necessary orientation information for those of you who wish to claim continual professional development points or units.

I have also included a written guide on how these credits can be earned and claimed. chapter two is all about laying the foundation for productivity and time management. Here we explore the concepts of time and its real value. We also take a look at prioritization, the illusion of results measured by volume. And we discussed the two pillars of time management in chapter three. We start breaking down the main contributors to waste of time. These time leeches are clearly defined and explained in order to create awareness and to ensure that you are conscious of the possible effects. chapter four is all about the anatomical sciences that can be related to time management with specific focus on your body and your mind and how they affect your ability to be productive.

chapter five dives into the established techniques that can be utilized to ensure that you effectively use your time and maximize your productivity. I also share with you what I refer to as the Kroner's or time yinyang or the balance of time, which in isolation has absolutely revolutionized the way in which I manage my own time. chapter six comprises some final wisdom I want to share with you. And chapter seven is a Book assessment, which is a requirement for professional development unit eligibility. The final chapter or chapter eight concludes the Book, and I share some final thoughts before seeing you into a whole new dimension of efficiency. So without further ado, let's start your journey of Crono Mastery.

Ratings and Reviews Please - Plus a Free Gift

I unwittingly started my time in management and productivity journey while I was still studying towards my bachelor's degree, and during the past few years of my career, I really made it a conscious study and experimental effort. I researched and practiced and put together what I believed to be the most important aspects anyone needs to master in order to take control of their time and to afford themselves the ability to actually live their time and not just squander it in service of their bad habits and others. I put this Book together in an attempt to share with you what I've learned and to give you the opportunity to benefit from my journey just as much as I did.

The only way I can know whether I am successfully transferring the knowledge I have gained is by getting your valuable feedback. Therefore, I beg of you, please take the time to give me your feedback, read the Book and please share your thoughts in a short review after the rating prompt. Your feedback means the world to me, and it is the only way that I can gauge the effectiveness of this Book and the applicability of its content. I hope you thoroughly enjoy the Book experience, and I really look forward to hearing from you. All the best. 4. PMI Professional Development Units Claim Procedure To claim your 5.5 PDUs after the completion of the Book follow these simple steps: 1. Visit the PMI CCRS website.

2. Log into your personal dashboard using your credentials. 3. Click on the "PDUs" drop down option and select "Report

PDUs". 4. Next click on the "Books and Training" option. 5. In the Provider and Book fields enter: "Master Time and Productivity Management: Take Back Your Life"

6. You can copy the following into the description field: "This Book teaches students everything they need to know about time management and productivity by teaching the background behind a productivity mindset, shining light on the aspects that steal most of our time and providing tried and tested productivity and time management techniques.

The Book comprises a balanced mixture of chapters teaching students the theory and structured/guided exercises aimed at priming the mind for the implementation of the techniques." 7. Enter your Book start and completion dates. 8. Enter your 5.5 PDUs into the three categories as follows: Ways of Working - 0.50 Power Skills - 0.75 Business Acumen - 4.25 9. Agree to the conditions and submit the PDUs claim. Note that you can only claim the 5.5 PDUs for this Book after the Book, including ALL the exercises has been completed and you are able to download the Completion Certificate. Should PMI wish to obtain proof of completing the entire Book you will need to furnish the completion certificate as well as the completed worksheets for the exercises. If you do not want to complete the exercises you can still claim 3.0 PDUs as follows: Ways of Working - 0.25 Power Skills - 0.50 Business Acumen - 2.25 To claim only the 3.0 PDUs you will only be required to keep a copy of your completion certificate.

Defining Time - What Does Time Really Mean to Us.

Before we get into the thick of things and most of the ultimate productivity tools and techniques, let's take a moment to philosophize about the meaning of time. In particular, they are about time. I really want to sink into the deepest crevices of your mind. For starters, I would argue that time is the single most finite commodity we have. Sure. The essence of time, from a universal point of view, is boundless. But from an individual perspective, there is a clear cap on the time you are graced with. Furthermore, regardless of your age, you will end up reaching before you turn into a seemingly insignificant speck of dust in the desert. That is history. We all have exactly the same amount of time in a day. 1440 minutes is all you get. Imagine the last joyful burst of laughter from your three year old daughter.

That absurdly funny moment you shared with your closest friend, you've seen the beauty of a special moment that you shared with your significant other. Put your fingers on your pulse. No, really. Put them. They feel each beat your heart gives the energy that surges through your body. Now, take a moment to come to the stark reality that each of these moments I just walked you through was the last of its exact kind you will ever have experienced. How is that for a punch in the gut moment of fleeting extinction ism? Fact number one. Time is finite, fleeting and precious, never wasted. One of the most common misconceptions I've heard from staff and students alike is the notion that time is money. In fact, for a large portion of my career, I was guilty of this fundamentally incorrect outlook as well.

Now, before you close your browser and shun my existence for ever uttering such absurdity as refuting the monetary value of time, listen to what I have to say. Almost every inconceivably successful businessman out there is keenly aware and actively preaches the dollar value of an hour and in some obscure measure of the definition of modern time, they may be right, but as easily as you can calculate your hourly wage. I can point out how obviously agitated, rushed late for filling. Most of these people with this viewpoint are. I'm not saying that I do not value the monetary value that can be connected to time. I'm just saying that it is not how I define how precious it is. I mean, how can money be the real value of time? I would argue that viewing time as money leads to a gross undervaluation of our time, because money is boundless and time is not. Time is finite. Time is life.

Once you realize that every second you waste is a moment of your life, you allow it to slip through your fingers. You really grasp the importance of time. And once you start living with the notion in the back of your mind, you can reach a new level of productivity, which ultimately still provides you with that monetary bonus that comes with effective use of your time. Fact number two, every grain of sand in the hourglass that symbolizes your existence is an endlessly precious second of your life, one that you cannot afford to slip through your fingers without meaning. With these two principal truths in the back of your mind, we will build a system, full time management that affords you greater productivity and profitability, while also enabling you to get the utmost living out of your time and life.

The Cumulative Effect

An important concept in time and productivity management activities is the cumulative effect in its most basic form, the cumulative effect refers to the aggregated or some effect of recurring activities over a period of time. Now, the reason I want to spend a quick minute on this concept is that it plays a major role in really grasping the negative effect that time leeches can have when looking at a single event in isolation. Its consequences may be seemingly negligible, but when you add various instances together and look at a holistic picture, it becomes an entirely different situation. The best way to visualize the cumulative effect is by considering the aggregated effects of a seemingly unnoticeable event. Let's say Jason is a smoker and Janet is not in order to collect his thoughts and satisfy his addiction.

Jason takes three five minute smoke breaks during the Book of a business day. And Of course, Janet takes none. She just keeps working. Jason is therefore spending a total of 15 minutes a day. Smoking 15 minutes seems like nothing when compared to the 480 minutes in a business day, and even less so when compared to the thousand four hundred and forty minutes you have in a day. But let's consider this from another angle. There are five business days and 52 weeks in a year, of which about 48 are working weeks. If you subtract annual leave, and that means that Jason is spending a total of 48 weeks, times, five days, times 15 minutes smoking instead of working.

The cumulative effect of his little habit is a staggering 3600 minutes, which amounts to 60 hours or seven and a half business days. Suddenly, it no longer seems so insignificant, does it, from this perspective? Jason is working a total of a week and a half less than janitors in any given year. It's absurd, right? Never, ever underestimate the aggregation of numerous small things. Now, I know there are benefits to short concentration breaks, and we will get to that later on in this Book. But the purpose here was to illustrate that many of the time, leeches that seem small before you grasp the concept of accumulation or actually really sucking immense amounts of time out of your schedule.

Time Management and What Can Actually be Managed

Although time and productivity management are the recurring and central themes of this Book, I want you to take a moment to think about the manageability of time. How can we manage time? How can we influence the quantity flow or movement of time? The short answer is we can't. When we refer to time and productivity management, we are actually referring to a time orientated subcategory of refined self-discipline and the formation of habits. In other words, improving productivity is not a matter of how we manage time, which can't be managed, but how we manage ourselves. Now, while on the topic of self-discipline and human habitual nature, there are two very specific things I want to bring to your attention. Habit formation and procrastination.

Firstly, improving management of yourself involves the process of forming new and better habits and whether or not you would like to admit it has information is not for those playing the short game. As with everything else in life, there is wide speculation on this topic. But research suggests that it can take anywhere from 14 to 256 days with a weighted average of 66 days to form a new habit. I know the spread is questionable, but the core message is clear. If you are going to improve your time management, you will self-manage. It is not going to happen overnight. Practice what you learn in this Book every day.

Tailor it to best fit your personal circumstances, and most importantly, keep at it. It won't happen overnight, and that is OK. But when it happens, it absolutely will be worth the effort that you put in. The second concept I want to spend some time on is procrastination. Now, I used to think that procrastination was nothing more than the embodiment of laziness. I was ever completely wrong. Procrastination is the consequence of your body and specifically your brain's internal reward system, which is a legacy of prehistoric survival instinct. Your brain really doesn't want you to suffer. In fact, it wants nothing more than to please you and reward you. And that is where procrastination comes in.

It boils down to an innate tendency to want to put off harder, less thrilling tasks for easier, more dopamine inducing tasks which provide you with instant gratification as opposed to long term value. If you are procrastinating, you're not lazy. You're just not motivated enough now that you're aware of what exactly procrastination is. You can overcome it by means of self motivation and a little projecting, connecting to that disappointed and stressed future self that will come into being if you keep on putting off that very important task.

Exercise 1: Building Self Discipline

This is going to be your first exercise in this Book. But as I mentioned in the introductory chapter to the Book, I really want you to commit to actually doing the exercises. That is the only way in which you can really benefit from what you're learning. The first exercise is all about building better self-discipline, which, as I explained in the previous chapter, is an integral part of improving your productivity. Starting tomorrow, I want you to do the following. Firstly, set your alarm clock about 15 minutes earlier than you normally would. And as soon as the alarm goes off, count back from three. And once you reach zero, immediately get out of bed. Do not lose the alarm. Do not lie in bed for a second longer than as far as I can count.

Believe it or not, this is a very simple but very powerful exercise. It gives your brain more decisive behavior. And it is a very effective way to counteract procrastination. And those extra 10 to 15 minutes in bed is nothing else than procrastinating behavior. Another benefit of this method is that you do not allow your brain to process how you are feeling. Just after waking up. There is no time for doubt, tiredness or simple laziness to set in. The second thing I want you to do is to eliminate all distractions from your morning routine. No social media first thing in the morning. No television, no radio, basically no electronic device related activities.

It is just going to be you. Your thoughts and this exercise. Lastly, I want you to make your bed before you leave the room, at the very least before you leave the house. This fosters discipline and allows you to start your day with a mini victory, which, believe it or not, has a major impact on your thought patterns for the rest of the day. Do these exercises for about a week and you should start noticing a difference in your self-discipline and motivation. The exercises are very simple and may seem too insignificant to make any sort of difference. But you're training your brain to improve your self-discipline and it will change your life if you really commit to it.

Mistaking Movement for Achievement

Probably one of the biggest mistakes almost all of us make when it comes to the productive use of our time is mistaking movement for achievement. The fact that a task needs to be completed and is perceived to be time and input intensive really does not mean it is actually worth doing. From my experience in practicing and teaching productivity techniques, human beings have a primitive psychological default setting which airs on the side of efficiency. I know I really have a tendency to make confusing statements. But here's the thing. Yes, efficiency is extremely important in the quest for productivity, but efficiency that is not structured around effectiveness is completely useless.

Let's take a quick look at the definition of these two terms. Efficiency is all about achieving maximum productivity with minimum wasted effort or expense, but efficiency in isolation is indiscriminate. In other words, it is not focused. Effectiveness, on the other hand, is all about the degree to which something is successful in producing a desired result. In other words, it is goal specific and focused. Consider the following scenario. Susan is the world's fastest reader, and she regions' punishing 3000 words per minute. She has been tasked with researching historical engineering practices to aid with the conceptual design of a bridge for a client who has requested that they want to design with a historical feel. Susan immediately starts reading up on engineering design, searching, modern engineering and architecture magazines and journals for information.

She can read these magazines at an unmatched speed, so efficient she is off the charts. Will this help her in solving the problem she has been tasked with? In all likelihood, it won't. Susan may be able to execute this task faster than anyone else in the world, but her focus is off. In other words, she is not being effective in our approach. Productivity, therefore, boils down to a marriage between these two aspects of applied time. Not only do you have to spend your time as economically as you possibly can. You also have to make sure that you spend it on the right activities. The ones that make the real difference, you need to prioritize, hit the big impact activities and leave the Carrión to the crows movement is not an achievement. Only movement in the right direction is. We will revisit this concept later in the Book when we start taking a look at the mechanics of prioritization and how it yields effective efficiency.

Exercise 2: Start Prioritizing

This exercise is all about priming yourself to start prioritizing. Think about your day in the office or in your study whether you're going to be working tomorrow. What are the things you absolutely have to achieve during the Book of just tomorrow? Now, think about what activities you will have to engage in to get through the day. Once you have a clear picture in your head of what is necessary for the day, I want you to isolate the one or two absolutely pivotal activities. These will be the one or two activities that will define you successful that day, the one or two things that if you only manage to get them done, will be good enough to call your day of victory. Start your day tomorrow with an absolute laser focus on these activities. Start with one and finish it in totality before moving on to the second. If there is a second, do not allow yourself to be distracted.

Keep your emails closed, your phone on silent and close your office door or put your earphones and you use. If you are in an open office, once you have completed your priority tasks, you can answer your emails and do whatever else you managed to get done for the rest of the day. The important thing is to start teaching yourself the value of prioritization, a concept. We will revisit later in this Book. Give this a try for about two working days and monitor what the results are. You'll be amazed at how this can change the way in which you approach your day at work. Feel free to share your experiences of this exercise and any of the other exercises in the Q&A chapter of the Book. Or you can send me a personal message to discuss your experience if you'd like.

The 2 Basic Principles of Time Management

Now that the foundations of time and its management has been laid, we can take a quick look at what I consider to be the two pillars of productivity time and productivity management is both upon two very basic principles, namely priorities and mechanics. We talked about the fact that movement should not be mistaken for achievement and that efficiency without effectiveness will still take you nowhere away, even though it will do so faster. How do we ensure that we are effectively applying our time simply by means of prioritization? Make sure that you spend your time working on the one or two absolutely most important activities that will get you closer to your ultimate goal.

And make sure you do it in a way that helps you circumnavigate or outrightly avoid the time leeches, which we will be discussing in the coming chapters. The second pillar of mechanics is all about techniques and methodologies that you can use to form productive habits in your day to day life. In other words, it's all about forming the habits that will help you effectively apply the knowledge you have gained about the years and nays of time management. We will take a closer look at these techniques in the coming chapters of the Book. Next, we will take a closer look at those leeches that you don't want anywhere near your fountain of time.

The Productivity Fallacy: Multitasking

How many people do you know that pride themselves on their abilities to multitask? Not only do I know several, I used to be one of them. I'm not saying that multitasking abilities are not something to be proud of, but I will say that multitasking is not doing the productivity levels any favors, even if by some miracle you are one of the very few people in the world who can multitask with some semblance of efficiency, you are still unknowingly wasting hours of your time, just as a side note. It is estimated that only about 2.5 percent of people in the world have the ability to actually multitask with some efficiency, and even they are limited to the extent in which they can do so.

You see, the thing is, multitasking is a fallacy. No one can really do two or three things at once while maintaining the necessary levels of concentration required to properly function during the execution of tasks. I mean, do yourself a favor and go to YouTube, a few cell phones while walking fails. It is absurd what people get themselves into by trying to text while walking. And these are two seemingly simple activities. What actually happens when you try to multitask is that you switch between concentration themes in regular intervals. And this comes at a significant mental cost. It is a concept known as context switching. And there is ample research available on the negative effects of context switching.

In particular, the psychologist Gerald Vineberg found that you lose about 20 percent of your productive time when switching between two activities, 40 per cent when trying to switch between three activities and a staggering 80 percent of your time disappears into thin air. When you try to juggle up to five tasks at the same time, to make matters worse, the average individual is thought to switch between activities in three minute intervals. It is no wonder most people feel like there isn't enough time in the day to get to everything. They are unknowingly committing productivity suicide by trying to juggle too many activities at a time when you have an important task to complete. Especially if it is one that requires a fair level of concentration and can be considered to be a challenging activity.

The single best thing you can do is to drown out all distractions. Forget about your other activities for a few minutes. Put your head down, focus and complete that activity before moving on to anything new. Unfortunately, most people cannot sit down and absolutely focus for a full eight hour working day. So there are definite limitations to how you can go about this approach. We will take a look at some techniques you can use to assist your brain with these concentration sprints later in the Book.

The Misconception of the Right Moment

I think it is safe to say that we all have some concept of how friction works. In physics, there are two main types of friction: aesthetic friction and kinetic friction, static friction related to the frictional force that has to be overcome in order to get a stagnant body of mass moving. And kinetic friction is the frictional force that has to be overcome in order to keep the body moving. Kinetic friction is always less than static friction. In other words, it is harder to get something moving than to keep it moving. You're welcome to do so. A quick experiment plays a relatively heavy object on the table now. Gently push against it until it starts moving and then move it a few centimeters or inches.

If you concentrate, you will notice that it takes more effort to get the movement started than it does to sustain the movement. And this is just one of the basic laws of physics. But the law is actually universally applicable to almost all aspects of life. And productivity management is no exception. More often than not, the hardest part of executing any given activity lies in starting the activity. And it is because of this fact that humans have created this illusionary concept of the perfect timing and waiting for the right time. The truth is, there is no right time. The best way to get something done is to start with it and iron out the kinks as you move along. I myself have a severe obsessive compulsive disorder.

And thanks to this little glitch in my brain, I used to be particularly guilty of waiting for the right time, the right time for an OCD person. Of course, after I had completely over-analyzed something and I'd spent enough time figuring out what could and could not happen, that I would have been able to complete the task itself. Luckily, I managed to overcome this through discipline and conscious decision making, and I cannot begin to explain how much I have benefited from it. Stop waiting for the right time. It won't come around. Start whatever you're planning now and you will find that starting was the hardest part. Once you have gained momentum, it is easy to continue.

Self Preservation and Avoiding the Uncomfortable

The human brain, one of the great marvels of the universe, something that is so profound and absolutely awe inspiring that there are several fields of science dedicated solely to single aspects of this magnificent piece of gray matter that falls or skulls. In most ways, our brains are the miracle devices that keep us alive and moving forward. And in some other ways, it can be our greatest crutch. This is where self-preservation comes in. It is an absolute must have reflex if we are to survive the harshness of the world. But we have to teach ourselves how to distinguish our innate abilities to unconsciously lean towards self preserving activities. Oftentimes causes us to avoid the uncomfortable, like the bubonic plague. Unfortunately, I've found that most often it is those uncomfortable situations that we are avoiding at a primal level.

There are also the activities that will contribute most significantly to the attainment of our ultimate goal. As humans, we have this tendency to use busywork, to rationalize our evasion of that awkward or most important task. We will tell ourselves that it wasn't possible to get to that task because we were too busy doing X, Y and Z. We do this purely because our brains are wired for self-preservation. Avoiding the difficult situation is easier, and not doing that most important activity can help us avoid the disappointment of failing at it. The thing is that prioritizing the important task and getting it done at whatever cost will most probably get you 50, 60 or even 90 per cent closer to your goal, whereas doing X, Y and Z usually result in a meager five or 10 percent.

These percentages are, Of course, fictitious, but the message is absolutely true. There are few things as unproductive as avoiding the bed because of anxiety or just not feeling like it. Learn to distinguish between required self-preservation and self-preservation tendencies that have absolutely nothing to do with preservation and condition yourself to take uncomfortable but necessary situations head on. Doing this alone will already have a major impact on your productivity and your life overall.

Exercise 3: Face the Uncomfortable

Once again, a very simple exercise, but one that is very powerful. As I mentioned earlier in this Book, time cannot be managed. We can only manage ourselves. So let's improve ourselves so as to better manage ourselves for the next five days. I want you to make a very conscious effort to do something uncomfortable every single day. I'm not asking you to pick a fight with an enemy champion, if you know you will. This groaning person in town. Don't try to 360 or personality choose activities that you personally struggle with, small as they may seem to others, and conquer them one at a time. When I started priming my brain to face the uncomfortable, I started by simply making constant eye contact with those who are more confident than myself. And I forced myself to face conflict situations instead of avoiding them.

And without setting out to do so, I managed to boost my self-confidence and learn that conflict does not have to be a fight. I learned to calmly face conflict and resolve it without letting flaring emotions take control of the situation. Whatever your weaknesses, or start small and face daily for this five day period, I want you to write down your challenge in the evening before you go to bed and evaluate yourself on your progress of the day. Make it a conscious effort and not a march of shame. Do not chastise yourself if you fail. Try again and keep trying. If you find yourself sweating as you prepare to face your challenge, that's a good thing. It is exactly that feeling that we are trying to learn to overcome.

Planning: The Misperception

I found while practicing teaching and implementing time management principles that people have a natural tendency to think of planning as not being real work. This is a major misconception shared by most people. I've come across people who do not want to waste time planning when they can rather spend that same time getting things done. At first glance, you might find yourself agreeing with this viewpoint. But let me tell you a little story to emphasize the impact of planning. About five or so years ago, my wife and I got invited to a baptism of one of our friend's firstborn. We did, Of course, accept the invitation, but at that stage, we didn't have our own children and consequently, we still enjoyed sleeping over the weekends.

Now, those of you with small children definitely understand the usage of the past tense of enjoy. Anyways, naturally, we overslept and only woke up about 45 minutes before the start of the service. Both of us frantically jumped out of bed and started getting ready for the event. I was, Of course, done long before my wife, who then asked me to take another look at the invitation and planned the trip in accordance with the map they provided. Knowing that we were late, I just glimpsed at the name of the venue and hurried ahead to get the car ready. About 20 minutes after waking up, we were both in the car and on the way to the baptism. About 20 minutes after we left our house, we stopped in front of the venue with five minutes to spare. Relieved at not being late, we proceeded to the parking area only to find it completely empty.

We were at the wrong venue at that very moment. My friend called, asking where we were, and he ended up having to direct me to the right . Needless to say, we were horribly late and I was public enemy number one. At least from my wife's perspective, refused to talk to me for about 90 minutes after we attracted the glaring gazes of disappointment from a whole venue full of people. The moral of the story here is that it more often than not happens that people tend to jump into the work because of overeagerness to show results. And in the process, completely neglect to plan and then having to face the consequences later on.

If I had taken literally one minute extra, I would have saved half an hour and not been late. The impact of planning cannot be overstressed. Stop looking at planning as a waste of time and realize now that spending 10 to 20 minutes planning your day or a large scale activity can save you hours of fixing avoidable mistakes or daunting in the wrong direction. Having a plan and a strategy gives you the advantage of knowing where you are heading. It provides you with a benchmark from where you can move forward and it keeps you accountable for the time you spend.

It also eliminates the need to spend time deciding on what to do next, which opens up some mental bandwidth, which you can focus elsewhere to improve your productivity. Planning creates focus and focus begets productivity. We will spend some more time on how you can approach planning in later chapters of the Book. For now, I want you to take the following words to heart. Never, ever start your day before it is finished. But more on that later.

Personal Neglect

As we work through this Book, you will notice a very distinct central theme, a recurring theme. I'm talking about the one that centers around you. You are the absolute fundamental key to your own productivity. You have heard me say this before and you will hear me say it again. Now, let's imagine for a second that you have just spent an entire 24 hours a week trying to circumnavigate the devastating aftereffects of a massive earthquake that hit your city. You are physically drained and on an emotional knife edge. You have lost everything you have worked for up until now. And you don't know where all your family members are yet. Now, imagine your supervisor calls you and demands you to complete a report that is due in three hours.

Do you think you'll be able to get any work done on this date? Absolutely not. I know that was an absurd exaggeration and it completely blows things out of proportion, but it does get a point across. And that point is that you are less able to work effectively when you are emotionally or physically distressed. Another way to look at it is by acknowledging that when it comes to time management and productivity, your energy level is everything. And energy is not limited to your physical energy, but also your emotional energy. You can master all the greatest productivity hacks and techniques in the world. But if you neglect yourself, you will only be able to produce a fraction of the results that you may actually be capable of.

If you want to improve productivity and you do not put consistent effort into managing your health, your physical and mental well-being, then I can tell you now that it will all be a wasted effort. And while we're on the topic of self neglect, I would like to urge you to really attend to your personal well-being, not only because you want to improve your productivity, but also because you deserve to get everything you can out of your time, not just more stuff done. Remember the opening chapter of chapter two? Time is precious, and every second it takes by the second of your existence that you will never have the opportunity to get back. So really, look after your personal well-being and never neglect yourself. You deserve better. We will take a closer look at combating personal neglect and the chapter on the human anatomy behind time management.

Distractions: The Twenty First Century, Your Friends and You

Oh, what a wonderful age we live in, the 21st century has become synonymous with extraordinary technological leaps. It has never been easier to be in contact with your loved ones to follow the day to day movements of your idols on social media, or to get that new gadget you've been eyeing for the past two months on a Sunday evening on Amazon while lying in bed. The information age and all that has developed from its knowledge, rich bosom has enriched our lives beyond measure. It has, however, also introduced some unimaginably detrimental Crono carcinogens or time carcinogens. For those of you not following carcinogens or agents with the capacity to cause cancer.

Yes, you heard me right. I'm referring to the miracles of the 21st century as Crono Carcinogens. With this, I'm not inferring that you should take up the Amish culture and divert your attention from any and all technological beasts. No, I'm just preaching caution. I mean, we all know that the sun and over exposure to it can cause skin cancer, but it is also the body's main source of vitamin D. Yes. Avoiding the sun your whole life could prevent skin cancer, but it could also lead to a myriad of other ailments due to the Vitamin D deficiency. Our natural response to the aforementioned is an unconscious balance between exposure and avoidance.

Most of the time, at least, this relationship we have with the sun, or at least the one we're supposed to have, is exactly the relationship I want you to have with the wonders of the 21st century and technology. Do not avoid it completely, but also do not overindulge to the point of detriment. Avoid the distractions that technology presents and your productivity will be better off for it. On the topic of distractions, there are, in my experience, three main factors. We've already touched on technology. The first and most dangerous of the three. The other day are your friends and you, Of course, by your friends, I'm really referring to people in general. Ever been in an open plan office where your co-worker just cannot shut up about their cat? And it seems like the inner voice is on a constant Dodge speaker.

Yeah. It really doesn't help your productivity, does it? Neither does that quick five minute request from your colleague just to run something past you. I'm sure you can think of an entire list of these types of small or large distractions that other people introduce into your day. The loss of the major distractions is me. And by that I mean you you oftentimes your own greatest enemy when it comes to productivity, jumping between tasks, remembering to call the dentist to make an appointment for your wife, while midway through that important report that you need to submit this afternoon, quickly checking Amazon to see if that new gadget isn't special yet. Yeah, you really need to stop interrupting you. Distractions are plenty, especially in the time we find ourselves in, and their influence on our productivity is immense.

According to a study conducted by the University of California, Irvine, it takes an average of 23 minutes and 15 seconds to get back to the task. That's twenty three minutes and 15 seconds that you lose once you have been distracted. That means that once you hit the zone and something distracts you, it will on average take you twenty three minutes and 15 seconds to get back into the zone. Absurd, isn't it? This means that omega three distractions, which I doubt would be the case for anyone I know, could mean a lot of an hour's worth of productivity. Be more mindful of the distractions you face on a daily basis and avoid them and so far as you practically can. We will take a look at a few simple techniques that you can use to reduce distractions later on in the Book.

Distractions Categorized

Now that we have Covid distractions and their primary sources, I think it is also a worthwhile exercise to categorize the main forms of distractions. We all know how dangerous stereotyping can be. And this is a statement that is no less true for distractions than it is for human beings. If you treat all productivity distractions the same, you'll probably end up being fired or wanting to fire yourself. Remember that a distraction is anything that hinders you from executing a task from start to finish. I find it very helpful to categorize these disruptions and treat each category with a singular type of mindset. The first category of distractions are what I like to refer to as profligate. The word profligate is an adjective which describes ridiculously extravagant or wasteful in the use of resources.

How fitting, right? These are menial, unimportant and little tasks that, through the help of accumulation, end up squandering our time without any form of measurable gain. Profligates include social media, surfing, emails, messages, phone calls and discussions pertaining to matters of little or no importance. Contrary to what you may be thinking, these distractions are not limited to the obvious things, such as telemarketing calls, spam emails, which is some reason people love to take a gander at, and the discussions about your weekend in the hallway. They also include ease of accessibility issues.

When I started my productivity improvement journey, I realized that there were days in the office that I was spending up to 80 per cent of my time, either answering manual emails or talking on the phone. The problem was that I was too accessible to some extent. People stopped thinking for themselves and interrupted me for guidance on the smallest of things. My answer to this issue was simple. I gradually started restricting my accessibility and hear me out now. To this day, I maintain an open door policy, and in the sense that I am open to discuss any matter that is perceived as pressing. It's just that people change their definition of pressing based on my limited accessibility.

I'll spend some more time on how you can implement this in your own living and working environments later on in the Book. For now, just remember that profligate or battled by means of access restriction. The second destruction category is something I call delegation phobia. This category of distractions include all those tasks that people, especially junior managers, refuse to delegate. Oh, never forget my first performance review at the very same firm. I ended up becoming a director just three short years later. I used to be a manic workaholic, spending upwards of 80 hours a week in the office. And as a result, I got things done. The question of at what cost was, Of course, something entirely different.

Nonetheless, my first performance review went exceptionally well with one little hitch. That being the following comment, exceptional workers should learn to delegate more and trust himself. Sounds like nothing, right, for the young, overachieving little idiot that I was. This comment was unacceptable. I was literally working myself to death and I was expecting a perfect review. But my inability to delegate was apparently a big issue. My supervisor mentioned that I could easily increase my output tenfold if I could just learn to master this one thing. Naturally, I tried delegating before and ended up having to redo everything anyway with my fingers burned. I ended up doing everything myself, and consequently I was delivering a fraction of my potential output at an enormous time of cost.

I know that my specific circumstances may be somewhat unique, but the core chapter that I learned is a universal truth. Put an end to that delegation phobia and you'll be absolutely amazed at the time benefit that you can reap. More on delegation later on in this Book. The third category of distractions are what I refer to as extortionists. This is a bit of a pseudo synonym, but it clearly reflects my sentiment on these distractions. They leverage perceived threat of consequence to take advantage of our time. They are unnecessary and even important disruptors that absorb our time under the guise of the importance and sometimes perceived emergency status without us even realizing that it is happening.

You know what I'm talking about? Those high importance tagged emails that pop up into your inbox every so often, the customer key tasks you need to attend to the phone call from your direct supervisor. Financial reporting, H.R. The administration state is reporting and the like. These tasks are recurring. They are necessary and unavoidable. Yet they are extorting you out of valuable time. You can't eliminate them, as that will probably lead to your own elimination. So how do we handle and urge vetch and trim? Beeching is a well known technique aimed at lumping similar tasks together and completing them all or working on them until the desired level of progress is achieved. Coming to me is all about optimization of task execution by backing similar tasks together and systematically developing improved systems of handling these tasks. You can shave literal hours in a week.

Overwhelm: When You Feel Everything is Just TOO Much

We've talked about 21st century technology and the distractions that have become part and parcel of the age we live and work in. What we have not yet gotten into is the psychological effects that the information inundation we have grown so accustomed to can and will lead to. I'm talking about overwhelm, that feeling that everything is just too much. The heaps upon heaps of information flooding your brain, making you feel like it's spinning out uncontrollably. That feeling you get when you are lying in bed, but cannot seem to fall asleep because you just cannot switch off the onslaught of anxiety that cripples your concentration while sitting behind your desk because you just don't know how you will manage to get to it all.

I am sure we have all at some point or another experienced this feeling of overwhelm. The problem with overwhelm is that it leads to a measurable decline in your cognitive function and ability to think and act clearly and rationally. Your head tends to start spinning, and the feeling has a tendency to externalize in the form of uncontrolled task switching, leading to a situation where you touch everything, yet nothing gets finished, which leads to further anxiety and overwhelm. The good news is that overwhelm is largely a function of perception. What I mean by this is that the extent to which you feel overwhelmed by emotion, work or information is caused by your perception of your ability or inability to calmly control the volumes you are being confronted with.

If overwhelm is a function of your perception, then beating overwhelm is a simple matter of changing your perception and your ability to deal with information overload. By far, the most effective method I used to overcome overwhelm was to stop relying on my memory, get the information out of your head and onto a piece of paper, and suddenly you already feel like it is more manageable than it was when it was all swimming in your head. Many refer to this process as a brain dump, which is defined as the act, or an instance of comprehensively and uncritically recording your thoughts and ideas on paper. Getting the information out of your head and onto a piece of paper gives you the perception of control and visually affirms that the information is actually finite and controllable. In addition to combating overwhelm, I also believe that there are several major benefits to writing down your thoughts, intended tasks and ideas. We will take another look at the benefits of writing it all down in a later chapter.

Managing Your Time Vehicle

We've already discussed the effects that personal neglect can have on your ability to actually manage your productivity levels. If you are neglecting your personal well-being, your productivity, as well as several other factors of your life will absolutely suffer for it. At the end of the day, time is like a river endlessly flowing forward, never changing direction and never stopping for anyone or anything. In order to effectively navigate the river of time, you need a suitable vehicle. The bigger the vehicle, the more successful you will be at navigating the river. The one and only vehicle you have for time management and productivity mastery is your body. Or rather, you'll be. What I'm referring to here is every single aspect that comprises your being and that includes your body, your brain and your essence. Therefore, I would argue that in order to master the art of ultra productivity, you have to master yourself both psychologically and physiologically, turn your being your vehicle into a speedboat, and you will be able to navigate the river with ease.

Personal Strengths and Weaknesses

The philosopher Aristotle is known for many profound wisdoms. But my personal favorite is the following. Knowing yourself is the beginning of all wisdom. I honestly believe that one of our biggest flaws is the human race, is the idea of social normalization and adapting ourselves to what we perceive to be our best selves from the perspective of outsiders whose opinion really counts for nothing. I thought of this chapter with a bit of a philosophical truth to drive the point home. You know who you are. You know your strengths, your weaknesses and the aspects of your personality that makes you you know, I want to challenge you to really spend some time to do some introspection. Think about who you are, introvert, extrovert or envy. That integrator or segmenter. Morning person or nido.

Now think about how you can use who in what you are to your advantage. If you're a nido, do not try to forcefully join the five a.m. club. Your Bonnies Croner top is not going to change because you wanted to. If you are an introvert, do not attempt to recharge your energy levels by surrounding yourself with people. If you are a segmenter, do not try to blur the rigid barriers you have placed between your personal and work life. Be who you are. Sure, you can learn new habits and adapt quite well to new circumstances. But the morning person will, without fail, always be better at early morning productivity than the nido.

And the night owl will always be more productive during the late hours when the morning person starts really losing steam.

Try to identify the activities in which you really excel, as well as the ones with which you really suck, and then keep doing the ones which you're good at and outsource your weaknesses if you can taste everything and only retain the good. This is as much true for life as it is for productivity. Do not attempt perfect emulations of the successful people you admire because their style, although amazing and effective for them, will not necessarily do anything for you.

Tailoring Your Strategy

In this chapter, I very quickly want to further build on the discussion about knowing yourself and using it to your advantage. There are endless personality aspects out there and even more combinations of aspects which makes each and every one of us the unique individuals we are. In fact, I would wager that the entire world population of seven point nine billion people, as at the time of compiling this Book curriculum, are in some way or another unique. Even if I wanted to, I could not possibly put together seven point nine billion Tailor-Made productivity strategies. Luckily, I have no desire to even try and attempt to do this, as Borromeo would say.

Not with 10000 men, according to this. It is folly. Sorry about that. I'm a big Lord of the Rings fan, and I just couldn't resist. But really, it would be impossible. And even if it weren't, it would not be very effective. That is the beauty of any system. It's a set of principles and procedures according to which something is done. In this Book, you are learning the background, the knowledge, the principles, the procedures part is yours to make your own. I want you to use what you've learned so far in this Book and what you are still going to learn and place it against the backdrop of the tapestry that is a you then tailor it, you need to make it yours and optimize your productivity in the way that best suits you. Your personality and your circumstances.

Psychology

I have experienced many terrible things in life and few of which actually happened. This quote from Mark Twain is to this day one of my favorite quotes on human psychology and one of the most empowering things I've ever read. I'm not going to bore you with the specifics, but I had a long history with depression, anxiety, and to this day, I still battle my absurd OCD. But this quote lifted the weight of the world from my shoulders. You see, I realized that life is nothing more than a string of experiences. And experiences are governed by perspective. Ever been in a situation where you in a bunch of fringe went out partying for the night and one of them was in a depressed mood? You may have all had the time of your life, and you talk about the experience to this day.

But the person was depressed at the moment, and experienced something completely different. Well, that's the perspective that I'm referring to. Once you realize this, you are in a position to implement the immortal chapter in the words of Mark Twain. Your mind is and will always be the single most powerful weapon you have. Condition your mind, alter your perspective, and the rest will start falling into place. The biggest favor you ever do for yourself is to exercise your mind to the point where just like any other train muscle in your body, you can use it to your benefit. Get into the right mindset and whatever your goals may be, you've already won at least half the battle.

Psychology and its impact on your ability to use your time productively and to do anything effectively really is a field in and of itself. And it's way too vast to cover in this Book. In fact, I might consider making a Book on just that topic somewhere in the future. There are, however, five important aspects that I do want to touch on in this Book. Number one, you are what you think. Believe it or not, the conscious mind only accounts for about five percent of your total brain activity. The other 95 percent is the subconscious, the realm of the unnoticed that exists with such profound influence on our lives. You cannot even begin to comprehend its power. You see, the thing is, your conscious mind influences your subconscious mind and vice versa.

This is true to the extent that you really do become what you actively think. Because that is what dwells in your subconscious. Make a conscious effort to foster a positive outlook on life and your ability to take it by the words will increase tenfold. Not to mention how your productivity will benefit. Number two, goal setting and visualization. I remember reading the book, Think and Grow Rich by Napoleon Hill. No, I didn't read the book with the intention of thinking of myself, rich, but rather to peek into the mind of a man who wrote a book in 1937 that to this day remains one of the top 10 best sellers ever in its category. There was one central theme that I walked away with, and that was the concept of setting high expectations and practicing gold visualization.

Now, at the time of reading the book, I was a lot more cynical in my outlook of the world, and I had an absolute disdain for any form of what I perceived to be pseudoscience, which to me was everything other than natural science and physics. However, I decided to give it a try. I set time aside to solidify my goals in life. And I did so to my new details of what I expected to achieve. And I started setting aside time on a daily basis to visualize my goals, to think what it would be like once I achieved them, and to actually experience the euphoria of attaining them. And although I have a ways to go before I achieve more, I am now a firm believer that this technique is worthwhile. Just by the way, one of the goals I had written down was to attain a formal senior managerial position by December of 2019.

And I was offered part ownership and directorship in November of 2019. Number three, stop complaining. This one and the next is rather simple, but important and impactful nonetheless. Stop wasting your finite energy pool to endlessly precious time on complaints. Just stop complaining. It really isn't that bad. Remember that brain bandwidth I referred to earlier in the Book while complaining takes up some of that bandwidth which you could be spending on other much more meaningful tasks. You are here listening to me talk, which means you are serious about improving your time management and productivity.

So stop engaging in what I've come to realize is probably the single biggest time wasting exercise in existence. It literally gets you nowhere. And once you stop, you will soon realize the immense benefits that simple actions such as this can have on your life. No. Four, Exercise gratitude. Sounds simple, doesn't it? I really thought I had this one mastered until one fateful morning at about 1:00 a.m., sitting around an open campfire with an old study body philosophizing about life. And he told me one of the most striking things I've ever heard in an attempt to school me on the value of moments and the gratitude we should rightfully bestow upon them. He said the following. Imagine the last thing your kids did that made you proud. Well, the last thing you really enjoyed doing with them.

Now, imagine that that was the last time you ever witnessed them doing that thing. With what profound sense of importance would you treat that moment if you knew it was the last you would ever experience of it? And it struck me to the core of my being to treat every moment in life exactly like that, like it is the loss you will have of the sort. Be grateful, really grateful, and do it every minute of every day. Number five, look after your mental health. This goes without saying, but an extraordinary amount of your energy comes directly from your mood, which is in great part governed by your mental health. Exercise your brain like you would your body, be mindful of the state of your thoughts and master your emotions. I strongly recommend some form of meditation to train your brain if you need a place to start. I would definitely suggest the waking up app by Sam Harris. Revelation in mindfulness.

Exercise 4: Psychological Priming

This exercise is all about priming your psyche for positivity and molding that power mindset you need in order to get the most out of yourself. The exercise is rather simple, and it has three components. One, limit your information intake to stop complaining, and three, start practicing real gratitude for the things you have. I want you to consciously do this for at least a week or two. After that, it should become a ritual. If you find that you are slipping back into your old ways, revisit the exercise and do it as many times as you need. I've personally made this a way of life, and the benefits have been countless. Aside from the fact that my mental well-being has improved tremendously, I also improve my relationships and overall happiness.

So the first thing I want you to do is to make a conscious effort to limit your exposure to the absurdly high levels of information we are bombarded with on a daily basis, especially anything relating to the news. I found that the news tends to be overly negative, and I always felt either mad or anxious after listening to a bulletin on the local radio or reading the headlines. So I completely cut it out of my life. People talk enough for me to be able to stay in the loop on the most important things. I also want you to turn off all your social media notifications and refrain from using social media except for a predetermined time slot. This does, Of course, not count if your job entails using social media.

In which case, I want you to challenge yourself to only do work related activities on social media except for during those predetermined time slots. Now, before you rally the mob and ban me from the Internet, I would like you to think about what I'm proposing. If you think about it, most of the information you're hearing and reading has some form of an impact on your emotional state. And it uses some of your available mental bandwidth. Yet basically, ninety nine point nine percent of it is outside of your sphere of control. It will contribute absolutely nothing to your goals, and it will bring you nothing more than to suck the poison out of your life.

And a wound that you never even realized you had will gradually start healing. The second thing I want you to do is cease any and all forms of complaining. When I started this practice, I found it useful to move my wedding ring to my right hand when I did my first complaint for the day. The goal was, Of course, to end the day with my wedding ring still on my left hand. You can do this with anything you'd prefer. You'll see a ring, a rubber band or a bracelet. Challenge yourself to get through the day without having to move the item from the side on which you started the day. Just to be clear. I'm not referring to getting out your frustrations. I'm talking about real and unnecessary complaining.

You can still tell you better half about the frustrations you experienced throughout the day. Just try not to fall into a rut of negativity. The last thing I want you to do is to start practicing real gratitude. People, we live in an age of wonder whether you want to accept it or not. Things have never, ever in the history of humankind been as easy as they are now. You have access to all the information you can dream of. Medical science has made leaps since the Middle Ages and our life expectancies have doubled. I know life is still hard, unfair and sometimes even cruel. But turn your focus to your personal treasures. If you have the kind of support for an absolutely rock star wife like I do. Be thankful for every day. If you have two beautiful children who lighten up your day like I do, they will be thankful for them. If you have a bed to sleep in, a roof over your head, water to drink.

The ability to walk, talk here and see if you have your health, if you still have your parents, if you have any of these things, you have something to be thankful for, something thousands of other people wish for every day. So for the period of this exercise, I want you to take three times slots during your day. Typically when you wake up during lunch and before you go to bed and write down the things that you are thankful for today. I'm serious. Write it down three times a day. Look at it and feel the gratitude you have for these things. If you start this exercise, is someone inclined toward negativity? Then I hope this will absolutely change your life. And if you're already positive, I hope this improves your positivity even further.

Physiology

To achieve the highest levels of energy your body is able to provide you with. It is important to not only tend to your psychological health, but also your physiological health. The better your health, the higher your energy levels will be and the higher energy levels, the better you are able to concentrate and use your time. Again, physiology is a massive field, one that is way too large to cover in great detail in a Book on time management and productivity. But just like with psychology, it is one that is way too important to skip all together. So I've decided to spend time on four specific aspects that, in my opinion, will make the biggest contribution to your productivity. Number one, you are what you eat. This is meant to be more figurative than literal.

Even though the literal meaning is just as true, what it really means is that there is power in what you take into your body, whether it's the air you breathe, the food you eat, or the fluids that you drink. Everything you consume has an effect on your health and your body. Some in more ways than you even realize when it comes to what you eat and drink. It's really simple. And maybe even a little annoying because we hear it almost every day. Adopt healthy eating and drinking habits and try as best you can to stick to a healthy index. Remember that a healthy diet is not limited to what you eat, but also when you eat. In fact, when you eat is an extremely important component of a healthy diet.

It took me years to get this right, but I ate at least breakfast, lunch and dinner. If you can, it is also a good idea to snack on fruit in between. I know it sounds simple, but for a long time I was so busy that the only meal at a time was dinner. The moment I improved my eating habits and ensured that my body stayed fueled throughout the day, my productivity improved dramatically. The 15 minute breaks I took at breakfast and lunch and to snack on a fruit in between was repaid in productivity by at least four times in time savings. Adopting healthy intake habits will benefit your health, your longevity, your energy level and your focus. Number to 70 percent of your body is made up of water. Yes.

A staggering 70 percent of our body mass is actually normal H2O. The one component without which there would be no life on earth. Our brains actually comprise about 75 percent water. So what do you think happens when your body starts dehydrating? Lots of water has a profound impact on your cognitive abilities. And studies have shown that there is a definitive link between dehydration and your ability to focus. Even low levels of dehydration, which tend to go unnoticed, can influence your ability to think clearly, and consequently it can and will affect your productivity. You need to be keenly aware of your hydration when you are engaged in productive work and the moment you feel your energy level unexpectedly dropping and your concentration slip. Drink some water.

You can even incorporate water breaks into the strategies that we will be covering in the next chapter. Remember, your body is 70 percent water. And if you want to use it to the best of its abilities, you need to make sure that that 70 per cent does not drop. Seriously, please do not underestimate this little tip. Number three, leverage exercise for improved focus. It's a well-known fact that the benefits of improving your cardiovascular fitness are myriad. Simply put, your cardiovascular fitness is a measure of your body's ability to transport your oxygen intake from your lungs to your muscles and organs. With that oxygen is needed in order for the muscles and organs to perform their function. Remember, your brain is an organ, too, and one that is just as reliant on oxygen to perform at its peak.

Improving your cardiovascular fitness improves your cardio respiratory system, which improves your energy levels and the efficiency levels at which your organs can function. You don't have to run a 10K every morning to benefit from this either. You know, your body and your exercise appetite. Go for brisk walks, get an elliptical machine and exercise while you watch your favorite series. Ride a bicycle with your children. It doesn't matter what you do. Just try to elevate your heart rate through some form of cardio exercise for about 20 to 30 minutes a day. You won't regret it. No fool sleeps. Sleep is probably one of the most underrated things you can do to improve your health, energy levels and focus. This is especially true for people like me who have small children in the house.

My friend, you have no concept of the idea of lack of sleep until you're raising children or if, like me, you have a little boy with absurdly poor sleeping habits. Anyway, sleep really is not necessarily something that is equally attainable to all. But it is something you need to start prioritizing. Studies have shown that the average adult needs at least seven to nine hours of sleep in order to function at a normal level. This is, Of course, only an indication and I suggest you read up on sleep cycles and do a few experiments with your own circadian rhythm and sleep cycles until you find your optimum setting. For me, it is six hours of sleep between 12 p.m. and six a.m. and believe it or not, that is my optimal amount of sleep, which was determined by means of quite a few experiments. Like I said, it will differ from person to person. The important thing is that you figure out what optimum is for you and that you do your utmost best to optimize your sleep.

Exercise 5: Psychological Priming

This exercise is very simple, and it may not even be applicable to you if you're not already actively engaged in some form of recurring physical exercise. I want you to pick an exercise that suits you, whether it is yoga, Pilates, running, cycling or brisk walking, and compared to your exercise, a minimum of three days a week for 20 to 30 minutes. That's all. People tend to think they are too busy to exercise. And for the first seven years of my career, I was no different but made time to consistently exercise for just 20 minutes, three times a week. And soon it will become a habit, and you will not be able to imagine your life without it. And as a bonus, you will improve your cardiovascular fitness and start reaping the benefits we covered in the previous chapter.

Understanding Of Productivity Management

The stage has been set and the previous chapters you have been armed with a keen understanding of productivity management and the real value of time, the activities that are robbing you of your precious seconds and the immense influence that you, the individual, plays in your ability to effectively improve your productivity. The Book curriculum was deliberately designed such that you are armed with a background knowledge you require to understand time, its management and your personal influence on it. Now, in this chapter, we will be exploring the tried and tested productivity techniques that you can employ to further improve your ability to combine effectiveness and efficiency when it comes to the expense of your personal time.

Remember that these techniques are not cast in stone, and their creativity and ingenuity in the execution and tailoring of these frameworks will, without any sliver of uncertainty, make all the difference in your ability to master them. It is your time you want to win. So do it your way. You will notice that this chapter has more exercises than the previous chapters, and it was designed as such with good reason. I want you to complete each of the exercises and measure the usefulness for you personally. And at the end, I want you to employ the strategy of testing everything and keep only the useful use of what you have learned and make time and productivity management your own. I sincerely hope you enjoy the chapter of the Book and that you make the best of the exercises and techniques.

The War on Distractions Part 1 – Profligates

In the next three chapters, I'll be sharing some strategies specifically put together to battle the three categories of distractions mentioned in chapter three of this Book. The three categories I am referring to are, Of course, the profligate delegation phobia and extortionists of time. Let's start off with the profligate. You'll remember that these are at core, unimportant activities that steal our time from us in order to deal with these little agreements. You need to employ a multifaceted approach which all revolves around a single principle, limiting access ability to start off. You need to instill a keen awareness in all those around you of your viewpoint on the value of your time, thus limiting your accessibility to others.

Now, by that I mean that you need to make sure your co-workers, friends and everyone that can influence your time at work, even your superiors are keenly aware that you are busy being effective and efficient and you cannot afford to lose precious time on menial things. Please don't become the office grouch whom everyone avoids. You can do this without ever having to lose their charming office personality of yours. In fact, I managed to almost completely eliminate chit chat and unnecessary meetings, calls and emails merely by instilling an awareness of how busy I am during working hours. And I did it while still maintaining the reputation of being an extremely approachable manager.

When people come into your office and ask to interrupt, you simply reply by saying at the risk of coming over is absurdly rude. I have to ask you if you could possibly send me an email. Have looming deadlines. And my head is swarming with things I have to get done. I want to give you a request, the full attention it deserves. And I'm afraid my attention span just won't currently allow it or anything similarly. Really. Just make sure that you politely emphasize that you are very busy and cannot afford to lose concentration on your current task. Keep at it. And it will become something like a habit in your office or whatever other working environment you find yourself in. Limit others' accessibility to you.

The same holds true for meetings, systematically create awareness that most meetings are not an efficient or effective use of your time and start avoiding meetings as far as possible. If ever you really need to attend a meeting, make sure the meeting has an agenda and that the problem that will be discussed in the meeting is predefined. Meetings are not a platform for problem identification. Also ensure that meetings are always time bound. The first principle again and a natural limit, other people's accessibility to your time. Next, you need to limit your personal accessibility to wasteful distractors such as your phone and emails. Start by switching off your notifications. That includes sounds and vibrations. There is nothing more distracting than that ringing sound.

When you are in the zone working at your maximum efficiency, not to mention all of these notifications were designed by behavioral specialists to be impossible to ignore. Not necessarily the notification itself, but the like subscribe, reply or whatever it may be that gives you that quick dopamine fix. Remember, every time you pick up your phone, when you are mad, focus on an activity, you will switch in context or unintentionally multitasking. And you know now what the time and productivity cost of context switching can be. Also, make sure to unsubscribe from any services there that will not serve your goal. We all have those newsletters and promotional emails we receive daily, but do not really spend time on a list for the purpose of procrastination.

Chances are that out of 500 promotional emails, there will be only one from which you can actually benefit. And I can promise you that the 20 per cent discount you are receiving is not worth the time costs due to productivity interruptions. There are, Of course, some subscriptions that are really beneficial. For me, these are subscriptions to knowledge enhancing services for these. I've created a standalone Gmail address, and I only check that at night during my leisure time. And yes, learning is a leisure activity for this net. You can do the same for any subscriptions that you really value. Just make sure you are not receiving these emails on your working email. The last step I want you to take is to make sure that your email address and phone are only used for important messages. This sounds like a repeat of the previous steps, but it is not.

This is all about creating awareness of your limited capacity to check and respond to emails and voicemails. Oh, yes, I may have forgotten to mention, but you may want to start screening your calls and allow most of them to go to a voicemail recording, prompting the caller to send you an email if it's really important. If it is really important, the caller will leave a voicemail message or send you an email. Make sure that you have a no BS policy when it comes to emails and other forms of communication. If it is not important, do not send a message. And this is not only applicable to people messaging you, but also to your messages to other people. Keep it short, sweet and to the point.

The War on Distractions Part 2 – Delegation Phobia

I don't know about you, but I know far too many people, my past self included, who pride themselves in the fact that they do it themselves rather than waste time waiting for the wrong end result. What they don't realize is that they are committing a cardinal sin in the pursuit of success and efficiency. And it comes down to the age-old idea of spending vs. investing. Delegation phobia stems from the fear of losing Short-Term Time. But it comes at the cost of significantly more long term time. Sure, you will be able to complete an activity much faster if you do it yourself and you do not have to waste time training in a new office. More on right or wrong. Think of it in terms of a long term outcome, just as you would with any other investment.

You can spend double the time today and save 10 times that over the next year. I struggled immensely with the idea of delegating, partly due to my perfectionism and because I maintained such a high intensity working life that I could not bear the thought of having to waste an hour teaching someone to do something that I can just do in half an hour myself as I gained more experience and my responsibilities grew. I soon found myself in a position where this simply wasn't enough time in a week to get through the mountain of unnecessary, self-imposed responsibilities. And I ended up working at least 12 to 14 hours a day, sometimes seven days a week. Then when it all became too much, I started to delegate some of the work.

The first one or two times, it took a little more than I was happy with. But at the end of the day, the work got done before I knew it. I was delegating the bulk of my time consuming activities, and the work was being done at a phenomenal rate and quality without really planning to do so. I ended up training people to alleviate my burden, and both parties were better or for it. I had more time on my hands to focus on more important tasks, and I managed to transfer some of my skills to someone who could now use them to further their own goals. I had unwittingly learned through forced experience the value of investing time over spending it and the immense power of delegation. Furthermore, I was also delighted to witness the fact that the delegated responsibility had on the employees. People are a lot smarter and more resourceful than we generally tend to give them credit for.

A little more responsibility was received with great enthusiasm and people started thinking more for themselves. And coming up with ingenious solutions to problems before I even knew the problem existed. Learning to delegate and play to the strengths of the supporting team members in our firm has absolutely changed my productivity levels and my life for the better. If you are not an employee in an organization with a staffing structure that you can take advantage of, then this still applies to you just as much as learned to outsource. And you will be surprised at the monumental value you can add to your freelancing business. Or one man shows with the additional time you can now invest in strategic initiatives. Simply put, human beings are more productive when they spend time on what they're good at or enjoy. So shed those unproductive hours you spend on activities that bore you by delegating or outsourcing them.

The War on Distractions Part 3 – Extortionists of Time

The lost destruction cure we will be taking a look at is the solution to time extortion, the tasks we are kind of forced to do at recurring and regular intervals that end up draining our time without us really paying attention to the aggregated effect. As mentioned in chapter three of the Book, my solution to dealing with the extortionists is by means of batching and trimming. Patching is normally done at predetermined or pre schedule times. And the premise is quite simple. By backing similar tasks together and completing them in an undistracted sprint, you are avoiding contact, switching, maintaining focus, and completing them much faster than you would have. You took them in dribs and drabs.

Start by deciding on fixed times during which you will tackle those recurring tasks. Often they have piled up a bit and absolutely refuse to spend time on these activities outside of your scheduled batching times. And when it comes to Beijing, I want you to remember that the only way in which you can deal with extortionists is by involving the popo. Yes. You heard the idiot behind the screen correctly. The popo. Only in this instance, the pope doesn't refer to the police, but rather an acronym which will help you circumnavigate the biggest extortionists of all. In my opinion at least, and that is emails. It does, however, apply equally to other recurring yet required activities. Now, the first P stands for predetermined intervals.

You need to determine when you will be checking your emails during the day, decide beforehand whether you will check or email two, three or four times a day. I personally suggest two times. The first just before lunch and the second about 30 minutes before you leave work. Never check your email first thing in the morning. This is your most productive time, and it is better suited to more important and productive activities. The first O stands for overly optimistic timeframes. You need to determine an overly optimistic timeframe within which you can check your emails. This can be 15 to 30 minutes, depending on the volume of emails you receive daily. The trick here is to make sure that you choose a time frame that is too short to handle your average email volume.

You will see why this is important later in the chapter. Just take it to heart for now. Put on a timer with an alarm to notify you when your time is up. The second P stands for pursuit of absolute completion. Challenge yourself to get through all the important emails and answer them before the timer runs out. When you first start using this technique, you can choose an inconvenient time to reply to the ones that you could not get. The idea is to really punish yourself for those that you couldn't complete. You will, with practice, develop email etiquette that will be concise, effective to the point, and still include the necessary professionalism.

Once you have mastered this approach, you really need to punish yourself for not finishing in time. Last but not least, who stands for the final? Onto the next thing. Once your time slot is up. Move on to the next important activity on your calendar. Be relentless and do not allow your emails, which are in essence the priorities of other people. To become a roadblock in your own productivity, using the proper technique will be quite hard at first.

But you need to be disciplined and you will develop the ability to effectively employ batching to conquer those recurring devils that allow your time to seep unnoticed from the hourglass. The dreaming portion of dealing with time extortionists is something that you will find happening automatically once you start employing the popo batching technique. You will start improving your approach to executing certain task types. And in the process, Dream adjusts and improves your ability to dispense with these activities quickly and effectively. It is worthwhile to also make this a conscious effort, analyze your approach to certain activities, identify areas of improvement and implement improvement strategies.

Exercise 6: Limit, Delegate and Batch

This exercise will cover the last three chapters on the suggested ways to combat the three categories of distractions. It is a two day exercise, but as with all the other exercises, you're more than welcome to continue with the practice. Once you've completed the exercise. Profligates are combated by limiting access. So I want you to use the attached sheet and identify your profligate, whether they are self-inflicted or caused by your accessibility to others. Once you have the most prominent, profligate identified, the next step is to identify the ways in which you are going to be enforcing its limitations. Depending on your most prominent profligate, this will include measures to limit other people's access to you and to limit your access to your self inflicted time killers. Delegation phobia is, Of course, combated by means of delegating and outsourcing. If you're like me, when I first started my journey, this will be a difficult one to overcome.

For the purpose of this exercise, I want you to identify two meaningful tasks, not just simple minded ones that you are going to either delegate or outsource. Over the Book of the next two days during which you'll be doing the exercise, although the tasks that you perceive to be mindless should also be delegated. The purpose here is to get over your phobia. That is why I want you to select meaningful tasks. Yet not ones that you know are too difficult to be delegated. Time extortionists are combated by betting here. I want you to think about your normal day at the office or at whichever place of work you spend, your 9:00 to 5:00 and think about those regularly recurring tasks, such as emails, answering social media posts. That is work related or any other recurring administrative tasks that you are faced with every now and then once they are identified. Choose a time slot and a time frame and batch these activities, lumped them together and conquer them in one fell swoop.

The Power of NO: A chapter from the Book of Steve Jobs

Focus is about saying no, Steve Jobs, five words and two letters to live by. I had heard people warning about the dangers of being a yes man before, but being somewhat of a people pleaser, I'd never really taken it to heart. I mean, what damage could saying yes all the time really do? Now, back when I was severely overworked and on the verge of collapse from fatigue, when I could not find the time to exercise, work and attend to all the social callings, when I was not able to walk from one room to the next without forgetting why I was walking in the first place, due to the sheer volume of information, my brain was feebly attempting to process. It was back then that I heard the warnings about. Yes. But I did not listen to them. Thankfully, my eyes opened, hearing turned into listening, and I came across the words of one of the pioneers of computing.

Steve Jobs was known for the fact that he had equal reverence for the things that he did not achieve. As for the things that he did, he was a man who understood the opportunity costs of saying yes to everything. A man who made no secret of the value of no. As Jim Rong once put it. Do not let your mouth overload your back. Learn to say no as frequently and to the point as you possibly can. You have no responsibility to produce a reason or an excuse. Just say no and put your priorities and goals first. Remember, whatever you may be capable of. You are still human and you have a finite capacity. Do not burden your back with the promises of your mouth.

Instead, focus on what you can carry and carry it well. This will serve your personal productivity more than you can possibly imagine, especially if you are in the habit of saying yes. Focus is about saying no.

Exercise 7: Emulate my Toddler

My two year old son absolutely refuses to do basically anything I ask him to do. I've been described as a strong willed and stubborn person, but I'm sure that I've met my match and my boy. He does sometimes have a point, though, doesn't he? He refuses to allow me to dictate his time, and he spends his time on the things that serve his goals. However simple those goals may be for any parent taking this Book. Whether or not we like to admit it and regardless of how experienced and smart we think ourselves to be. There are chapters that we can learn from our children whose minds have not yet been corrupted by the world for at least the next two days. I want you to take a page out of the book of my two year old who refused to do anything that does not shoot your schedule or serve your goals. In fact, just say no to any request, only giving way when there's a threat of being fired. This, again, seems like a simple minded exercise. But like most of the other exercises, this one also serves as a primer to rewire your thinking.

Thinking on Paper

We've touched on the concept of limited bandwidth, and now I would like to expand on this. Most of our bodies' resources are finite. At least we have a daily capacity in terms of our energy and output capabilities. This fact also holds true for our brains. We have only a finite mental bandwidth. We can allocate to processing information, remembering tasks, handling decisions and running through all the other minutiae that forms part of our daily lives. So why overburden your brain by relying on what you think is your amazing memory? Even if your memory is that amazing, you are still taking bandwidth availability away from important activities and allocating them to a memory that you do not really need to rely on into the concept of brain dumping.

Write it all down. Your ideas, your appointments, your important activities that you need to attend to your goals, your thoughts and aspirations. Put it on paper and get it out of your mind. Doing this will bring a new level of clarity into your life, one that you may have been unaware of for many years. In addition to removing the fog of information clouding your thoughts, you will also find that it brings a sense of control. If it is no longer swirling around in your head and you can see it in front of you, it becomes measurable and achievable. Which in turn reduces your stress levels and further promotes productive use of your time. Don't just take my word for it. Sir Richard Branson, well-known billionaire, philanthropist and recent space traveler, absolutely swears by his notetaking.

In a 2006 interview, he was asked to rank the five most valuable tools in his climb to success. He gave only one notebook, in his words. I could never have built the Virgin Group into the size it is without those few bits of paper. The level to which you want to implement this is fully up to you. You can take up journalling or just comprehensive note taking, but make sure of three things, namely, take note, do it on paper and in a bound format. And create a system that you can easily navigate at a later stage. I've already substantiated the importance of taking notes, getting information out of your head and putting it on paper. Now, I will argue for the other two points.

Writing on paper has been proven to improve your knowledge, retention and perception. Studies on this effect have been undertaken by various universities, and the outcome always points to pen and paper being the single best medium for notetaking when physically writing. While you listen, you are employing visual, auditory and tactile mediums all at once. And you usually cannot write as fast as the speaker talks. So you are also processing and interpreting the information so that you can capture only the essential core aspects of what is being said. You're welcome to go ahead and read the Harvard article on the topic of low tech note taking. I've included a link to the article in the attached downloadable resource. This does, Of course, not only account for classroom application, but is applicable everywhere and anywhere else.

The reason why further advocate that your notebook's should be in a bound format is simply because you will only have one thing you need to remember to carry with you. The loose pages can't go missing. And it is easier to implement a multipurpose notetaking system in an all in one format. Creating a custom made system that enables you to easily navigate your note at a later stage is also extremely important. There's no sense in jotting down your thoughts if you're just going to leave it at that. Again, customization is key here. But I personally prefer a leather bound A5 size notebook that I carry with me most everywhere I go. I find tags in my notebook, one for things I need to remember, one for thought, one for ideas, and one for things I come across that I believe merits further research and reading.

The Lost is a general tag to which I allocate things, which I'm not able to categorize in the moment at intervals during the day. I scan through my things. I need to remember a list, and I schedule the appropriate time for these activities in my calendar. I also scan the general notes every now and then and organize them as need be. The thoughts, ideas and further research chapters are there for me to go through at leisure or whenever I remember that I had an idea, but I cannot exactly recall what the idea was. I usually work on these items at night when I have time to calmly think them through. Granted, I'm sure my notes pale in comparison to subbranches, but taking notes has definitely given me the ability to remember more, to process my thoughts with greater clarity, and just getting rid of the feeling of absolute powerlessness stemming from the haze that used to encompass my thoughts. By the time I reached five in the afternoon.

Exercise 8: Empty Your Mind on Paper

The purpose of this exercise is just to get you started on the road of thinking on paper. I already gave you an overview of how I use my notebook to record basically everything in my life. And I genuinely want you to adopt this practice in your life. But I cannot tell you what format will work for you. You can use your smartphone, a notebook or an example and just start writing things down and your brain will thank you for it. Now, for this exercise, I want you to download the exercise aid resource sheet and do what is commonly referred to as a brain dump. It simply means that you need to get everything that is draining your mental energy and the back of your mind out on paper. You need to write down everything you can think of that you need or want to remember. Just get it all out on paper.

Start with the immediate actions and then go deeper and longer-term. You can categorize it all into daily, weekly, monthly and annual tasks or use whatever format will suit your personality type and circumstances the best. Nothing is too small to note, nor is it too far off. If you're anything like me, especially back when I started with these practices, you will possibly be quite overwhelmed. And chances are that you have way more on your plate than you feel you can handle while doing this exercise. You will realize that this activity will bring you a sense of comfort and relief. Suddenly, it is no longer a vast ocean of unorganized information throbbing through your head. You wrote it down. You can see it, quantify it and defeat it. It is much easier to make a plan when you can see the components. And this exercise is a great way to battle your overwhelm.

Planning: Create Clarity and Banish Uncertainty

Never start your day before it is finished. We ended the chapter on the misconceptions of planning with these words. Now let's take a look at how to implement them, planning your day, your week, or even your year as a greatly underrated tool, which you can leverage to increase your productivity. There are various ways in which you can approach planning as a productivity tool, but I suggest a very straightforward and simple system consisting of a quick planning session at the end of your day and a planning session at the end of your week. Why plan at the end of your day? Because never start your day before it is finished. In addition to the clarity, calm and control you get from planning, doing tomorrow's planning before you knock off today has the additional benefit of relieving the stress and anxiety, usually accompanying the uncertainty of the day to come.

And it gives you the power to actually recharge and switch or when you're at home with your family and loved ones. The same holds true for planning your week in advance on a Friday before you leave for the weekend. For daily planning, I suggest you schedule about 15 to 20 minutes at the end of your day during which you can work through your notes and process your entries for the day. Schedule any items that will require action during the Book of the next day and write down any additional thoughts and activities that you deem necessary. Have a look at any unfinished tasks for the day and reconsider their priority and whether you can outsource or delegate them. If you decide to delegate, send a quick email, an instruction to the intended person before you leave work.

If you decide to complete the activity yourself, reschedule it at an appropriate time in your calendar. Go over your calendar for tomorrow and familiarize yourself with the entries you previously made. There is nothing worse than being surprised by a meeting that you scheduled yourself. Now that you have a clear idea of how you are going to conquer tomorrow. Go home and really take in the time you have at home with your loved ones instead of wasting it continuously wandering about unfinished business at work for weekly planning. I suggest you schedule, say, about 30 to 40 minutes on a Friday afternoon as the last thing you do before you leave for home after a week of productive work during this planning session.

Review the week behind you and create an outline for the week to follow. The activities are basically the same as for daily planning, except that weekly planning is done at a high level. Check your calendar and familiarize yourself with your pre scheduled responsibilities for the week ahead. Work through your notes and add calendar entries for the items that require it. Think about what you want to accomplish for the coming week and create a broad weekly layout that will serve your goals once again, reduce your overwhelm and do away with uncertainty so that you can really enjoy a carefree weekend and recharge that very important reservoir of energy so that you can take the coming week head on and give it the best you're capable of.

These are extremely simple principles, I know. But you will be amazed at the clarity that it can provide you with and how this sense of purpose will improve your productivity simply because you have a plan and you have banished the uncertainty and associated anxiety that steals your efficiency. Now that you have cleared some mental bandwidth, it can be allocated to much better suited activities that would better serve your goals and objectives, as Warren Buffett once said. Someone is sitting in the shade today because someone planted a tree a long time ago.

Scheduling vs To Do Lists

Here's a real clincher for you to do list is where important work goes to heart and ends up like the grape that fell and rolled underneath your fridge. Come on. You know exactly what I mean. You see it fall and it was just too fast for you to stop it. You end up thinking, I remember it there and just take it out tomorrow. Next time you are spring cleaning the house, you find a shriveled up that looks like it was placed there by the founding fathers. And they're supposed to be featured in the Museum of Natural History. Yes. To do lists or the equivalent of a slow and painful death for your important tasks.

There are a myriad of psychological reasons why this is the case. One of the most prominent being that we all have a subconscious tendency to urge towards the side of marking the many rather than the big. It makes you feel so productive when Marcall tends to list items in the stretch of two hours rather than marking that one big game changer. The truth of the matter is, however, that the one task you have been avoiding is worth more than 10 times the 10 you just crustal. In addition, traditional To-Do List does not make provision for prioritization. So your important and minutiae tasks all end up on the same list in no particular order and with no clear impact of completion.

And to me, probably the main reason why I absolutely despise traditional to-do lists is that it is a breeding ground for anxiety. And by now, you are well aware of the detrimental effect that that unwanted stress can have on your ability to productively use your time rather than using to do lists in an ill fated attempt to create a misconceived plan for your days. Use a well-organized calendar and actually schedule time for your activities. This is a technique commonly known as time blocking, and it is a productivity secret employed by many of the world's most successful and richest people. It works especially well with the notetaking principles. We Covid in the thinking on paper nature, as well as the daily and weekly planning techniques.

Put everything you need to do on your calendar, and if it is not, they act as though it does not exist. I'm not saying you should implement a completely rigid schedule. In fact, doing that would probably be just as good as not implementing the technique at all. The idea is that you only foresee activities if they are scheduled. But you can still maintain flexibility in order to afford yourself the opportunity to deal with emergencies. The best way to build flexibility into your schedule is to schedule regular 15 minute buffers and the occasional hour or two in a week to allow yourself to process the events up to that point and deal with emergency matters.

If something really big and unexpected happens, you can always reschedule your other tasks. This approach helps you to make real, measurable commitments, and it is a great system for keeping those commitments. One thing to remember when using scheduling rather than to do list is the fact that you cannot possibly do everything. Prioritize. Choose the most important and impactful tasks and make sure they get done.

The Pomodoro Technique

The Pomodoro technique is quite a well-known time management system that was developed by Francisco Cerrillo in the late 1980s. It's a simple and easy to implement technique that is centered around short work sprints with breaks in between. The technique basically centers around the common shortfall of human concentration. That being our inability to really effectively concentrate for long periods of time. The basis of the technique, as popularized by its creator, is that you pick a task that you will focus on, set a timer for twenty five minutes during which you will focus solely on the selected task. And once you have completed the twenty five minute interval or Pomodoro, you record your progress and take a five minute break to recharge your brain after you've completed four Pomodoro.

You should take a longer 15 to 30 minute break to fully restore your capacity to focus. In addition to the Pomodoro intervals, the technique also involves the following three very simple rules. Rule number one involves breaking down complex tasks into smaller, more manageable components, typically small enough to be completed in no more than four to five minute sprints. The second rule is based on the principle of batching and involves putting sets of small tasks together in order to fill a 25 minute sprint. And the last and most important rule is once the time starts, you do not stop until you hear the ding. Do not stop at Sprint to check your email or your phone or anything of the sort.

Luckily, you have already tended to this issue by eliminating the three categories of distractions from your working environment. Do not let the simplicity of this technique influence your opinion on its effectiveness. The technique really works because it counteracts some of the most basic side effects of the human condition, namely our distractibility and our tendency to lose focus when we try to concentrate for two long periods at a time. The technique has three very basic advantages. Firstly, it makes it easy for us to stop putting something off and just start with it, because you are breaking tasks down into smaller, more actionable units. You are also breaking through the wall of perceived complexity.

And in the process, staving off the natural procrastinating behavior we all fall victim to you. Secondly, it effectively combats distractions by forcing our brains to keenly focus for short sprints at a time with the reward of a break at the end of each sprint. This effectively requires our brains in much the same fashion as the trigger ruchi reward system popularly recommended for habit formation. And lastly, the technique turns your productivity into a challenge for continual improvement, working becomes a game, especially for the competitive in nature. Because with each Pomodoro, you unwittingly try to beat the high score you set in the previous round. Who said working productively had to be boring? This is a great technique, but in its basic form, it has some obvious shortfalls.

You have to be very realistic in your implementation of the Pomodoro technique. Do not try to structure your entire day every day using this technique because it is not universally implementable. Furthermore, the technique was developed specifically with a 25 five split, which I believe to be a great starting point. But the technique lacks motivation for personalization, and it does not take into account the effect of individualism. Test various sprint and break links sticking more or less to the ratio of sprint to break. In other words, if you're going to do a 50 minute sprint, then take 10 minute breaks. Taste the sprint until you identify your personal sweet spot and then use it accordingly. I find that the Pomodoro works particularly well with my task batching. And depending on your working environment, you may find different implementations that suit you best.

Exercise 9: Use the Pomodoro

I don't think I have to say much to explain this exercise. I want you to try the Pomodoro technique, at least for your next day at work. Follow the guidelines I provided in the previous chapter and implement the technique at work. Put a timer on your phone, your browser, or use your smartwatch. You can start with the traditional twenty five to five minute work sprint and break intervals and see how it works for you. You're welcome to adjust your work, to break time ratios and increase the intervals as it best suits you and your type of work. I would, however, suggest you do not go over a 15 minute work sprint with at least a 10 minute break.

The important thing is that you quickly preplan the tasks and that you do not allow any form of distraction during a Pomodoro sprint. If you work in an environment where you are isolated, just remove your distractions. If you are working in an open office, set up to inform your colleagues that you are going to do a productivity experiment and either get them to join in or put your earphones in. I'm sure you will be surprised by the level of efficiency with which you can tackle a task when you use this technique.

Prioritization and the Pareto Principle

Everything I've taught you up until this point was absolutely applicable and worth learning. And I hope that you will attempt each of these techniques and time management wisdom's at least a few times and use what suits your personal style and situation the best. The following three chapters are over the cream of the crop. The information I will share in these three sessions are what unequivocally changed my relationship with time and what gave me the freedom to pursue not only the 21st century expectations of my time, but also the real value of my time, the value of life. Up until now, you would have picked up on the fact that I have a keen appreciation for the fact that time and productivity management techniques are not a one size fits all solution.

And I actively preach tailoring and making it your own. This concept of tailoring remains just as true for the final conditions of this Book. Now, without further ado, I would like to introduce you to the Fred Operato. A 19th century engineer, economist and philosopher, a man that revolutionized the field of economics and the effects of individual choice. If it sounds like I idealize this man whom I've never even met, it is because I absolutely do. For he has, almost 100 years after his death, completely changed my relationship with time and choice as a whole. And here's how the burrito principle, also commonly known as the 80-20 rule or the law of the vital few.

Simply put, this universally applicable law states that roughly 80 per cent of all consequences hail from roughly 20 percent of all causes. In other words, the vital few important factors influence the bulk of the outcomes at the time of these research. The burrito principle was mainly attributed to economics and the distribution of wealth in Italy. In other words, 80 percent of the country's wealth was possessed by 20 percent of its population. Mankind has, however, since realized that this principle can be applied to almost all aspects of life. In business, 80 percent of sales usually come from 20 percent of the clients in sports.

20 percent of the training exercises usually account for 80 per cent of the gains in computing, 80 percent of the bugs stem from 20 percent of the code. The examples of the applicability of the Perretta principle are boundless. So why not introduce this principle into your time management system and your life as a whole? I promise you that you stand only to gain the 80-20 ratio per say is not a golden nugget here. It is the idea that it embodies that you need to take to heart. It can be nineteen ninety five, five or seventy five, twenty five. The point remains that the vital few influence the majority. And it is here that the epiphany of personal, professional and business optimization lies.

And boy, is it universal. You can apply this principle not only to your productivity system, but also to your friends, leisure activities, daily menial tasks, yardwork, work, stress management, etcetera, etcetera. Ask yourself what 20 percent of your problems are causing 80 percent of your stress? What 20 percent of your day to day activities contribute to 20 percent of your happiness. You get the idea, right? So when it comes to time management, it is quite simple, is it not? What 20 percent of activities will yield 80 percent of your desired results. At its core, the application of the 80-20 principle is all about prioritization. And prioritization is the link between efficiency and effectiveness. Analyze what you are doing, what you have to do, and what you want to do.

Analyze your life goals and your actions. This is to achieve them. Analyze what you spend your time on when you are taking time off. Identify the vital few things, the most critically important activities that will bear the most fruit and relentlessly place your focus on those activities. There are hundreds of things we feel we absolutely have to do during the Book of every single day. But there is only one or two things that will, if completed, make the entire day feel like a roaring success. Regardless of the state of the other 99 or 98. Activities develop a vital few minds and look at everything in your life through the lenses of this new mindset of yours. You will be surprised at the universality of this principle and the incredible productivity gains that it will provide you with. This mindset will also serve you well, far beyond the confines of the use of your time.

Parkinson's Law and the Magic of Deadlines

It's the last week of March during my graduating year as a civil engineering student. The South African summer is just giving way to fall and the weather is superb. I was just surprised by my then awesome girlfriend, now amazing wife, with an extravagant, self-made buffet on the balcony of my room in the student union where we both lived. I was in for an evening of treats. Great company and some well-deserved time off with the only person I wanted to spend it with. I'd just taken the first bite of a beautifully red strawberry buried so deep in Balwant sauce that my girlfriend made that only the stem was visible.

When I got a call from one of my study buddies. Glass shatters the city development simulation assignment. Responsible for an absurd third of our semester, Mark had been corrupted beyond repair. The day before, we had to submit this 30 to 40 page report summarizing a week's worth of statistical simulations and work. Long story short, after trying everything humanly possible to recover the corrupted document, I had to leave my girlfriend on the balcony to share the spread of the delicious treat with another one of our Comune friends. While I jumped in the car to race off and meet the rest of our three person study group to try and save ourselves from the pain of having to add another year of studies to our lives. Yes, the engineering faculty was that strict assignment. Not in the second.

The deadline is over. It's better not next year. And one less assignment for the chapter to suffer through. We had spent two weeks writing up, editing and finalizing the report. We had just lost to the evils of technology, and now we had a meager 18 hours beforehand. This meant that we only had about 15 hours to complete the report because we still had to print and bind it off campus and hurry back to hand it in without overthinking anything. We sat down, rotating between typing responsibility, simultaneously narrating a report like a practiced choir. About a dozen Red Bulls, several packs of cigarettes, a stress relief and an intense all-nighter. Later, we had a completely new report, one that we actually felt was better than the original.

We handed the report in on time, and as all good students do, we proceeded to the closest watering hole to celebrate our triumph. When the grades came back, we were surprised to find that we had managed to score a distinction for the assignment, and it was some of our best work for the semester and couldn't close. The moral of this short story lies in the magnificent wonder of the looming deadline. We were able to complete in 15 hours what had previously taken us more than two weeks of hard work to complete, and we had done so to equal or maybe even better quality. Why? Because we had absolutely no choice but to sit down, focus and complete. There was no time to overthink.

No time to overcomplicate. No time to waste on small, insignificant things which would have actually added no value. Only time to focus and get it done, lest we want to explain to our parents or bursar's why we would suddenly need a hell of a lot of extra funding to complete our degrees into Parkinson's law, which states that work expands to fill the time available for its completion. A law that found its origin at the hands of Northcote Parkinson, a man who had witnessed firsthand the detrimental effects of bureaucracy and the limitations of the concept of working harder and more rather than smarter and faster. This so-called law is actually a verbalized observation of another one of those human conditions. We can either choose to conquer or allow it to run rampant in our lives.

The more time you have to complete a given activity, the more the activity will increase in perceived complexity and the harder you will work to achieve the same quality of end result in the endless pursuit of the next adrenalin hyped fanfics. I had subconsciously applied this law to the entirety of my bachelor's degree studies, and in the process adopted a mindset of putting off work until the last possible, practically achievable second in order to devote my time almost solely to the experience of the student life. And although there are some who could not believe it, I'd managed to always make the cut. And I graduated within the minimum four year study period for a civil engineering degree.

Granted, my approach through the application of the law was fundamentally flawed in that I postponed to the last possible second. But there was some method to my madness in that I allotted practically achievable absurdly short deadlines to my work. In my later more experience years, I revised the approach just a little. Instead of postponing to the last second of an unnecessarily long time for completion, I just imposed a personally set deadline on all the work I had to complete. As a consequence, I started working smarter and faster, rather than harder and longer, simply because of the psychological hack I was employing in my day to day life.

The key here is, Of course, to remain within the bounds of the achievable. It would be ludicrous to assign an hour deadline to a 100 page financial report, just as it would be an absolute waste to assign a six month deadline to it. You could not possibly write 100 pages in an hour, and by attempting to be that unrealistic, you will actually be acting to your own detriment, not benefit. Give yourself aggressive but achievable deadlines to avoid doing busy work and force yourself to be productive, but always keep within the confines of reality.

The Jinjang of Time Management

The two most valuable weapons in my time management warchest have now been laid bare, prioritize, adopt a vital few mindset and always make sure you're directing your focus to the 20 percent of activities that will yield 80 per cent of the results. Set aggressive deadlines. Exploit the human condition by applying law and making sure you do not allow tasks to grow and perceive complexity. Now, there is one last concept I want to introduce you to. And it is not another battle tested technique, but rather the realization that sometimes the combined effect of two things in balance can be significantly greater than the sum of the individual effects. This is called synergy to make the most of principle and Parkinson's law.

You need to achieve what I like to refer to as the yin yang of time management, or very simply put, the balance between Berettas principle and Parkinson's law. These two principles complement each other perfectly. Make sure you are limiting your work input only to the critically important activities and limit your time available to complete your work so that you are forced to place emphasis on only the critically important activities. Furthermore, you can use what you've learned in this Book and from other known techniques to help you achieve this yin yang or balanced status.

Find the most important activities and schedule them in your calendar with clear and aggressive deadlines. Ensure that you create a workspace that is free from the distractions that plague our modern society so frivolously. Use your own duration tailored pomodoro technique to make sure you utilize your mind and body to the best of its capabilities. When doing sprints on the identified important activities, find your productivity balance and maintain it with what you have learned here.

Exercise 10: Find Your Balance

The last exercise of this Book will not be like any of the others. I'm not going to challenge you to try something for a week or two just to prime your mind and measure your results. This exercise is not just about creating awareness or removing small mental hurdles. This exercise is a lifestyle challenge. Go back and listen to the chapter on the value of time once again from this point onward. I want you to deeply reflect on what you have learned in this Book and what time means to you, how precious and wonderful every second that you are graced with really is, and how important it is that you learn not to squander this gift of life. Go and find your balance. Make it a conscious daily or weekly event to experiment, renew, adapt, improve and adjust the techniques and philosophies that you've learned here. Make it a lifestyle, not just a workplace philosophy. Take back your time and enjoy your hard earned winnings. I wish you all the best on your journey to self discovery. And I truly hope that you will enjoy it as much as I did and still do.

Test Everything and only Retain the Worthwhile

In this chapter of the Book, I'm just quickly going to share with you some final nuggets of wisdom. The Book already contains insufficient detail, the core knowledge that you need in order to become the productivity machine you want to be. But hopefully these final nuggets will also serve you well, test everything and retain only the worthwhile. I want you to keep this idea in the back of your mind as you formulate and construct the time management system that suits you and your unique circumstances the best. Remember, none of what you've learned in this Book is cast in stone. And as much as I would like to, I cannot give you the solution to a problem that is uniquely your own. Balme has already highlighted that such a task would be folly. Take the time to test everything you've learned in this Book. Adjust the core principles in ways that suit your personality and style based, shed any unnecessary weight or redundant practices, and keep only the principles that you find works best for you. Create your own lean time management system and conquer your time.

Enough is Good Enough

You are here listening to me because you want to win back your time. Now, I would guess that I'm correct when I assume that this factor alone makes you quite an ambitious person. Why else then, how to master your time? Ambition is great. It's one of the best motivators out there. And it keeps us in the path of never ending personal improvement. But it can also work against us many times. Our ambition drives us to want to do way too much. Even if you mastered the art of productivity and you use your time as efficiently and effectively as humanly possible, you are still stuck with a measly 24 hours in every day. Remember this and learn that enough really is good enough.

Definitely. One of the more difficult things for me to master was the art of walking away and accepting that I've done what was necessary, what I could do, and that nothing more is needed. I also want you to remember that just because you decided to start something and just because you've spent some time on the activity does not necessarily merit continuing with it. Sometimes we have to re-evaluate what we are busy with. And as soon as we realize that it is not in service of our goals, stop and walk away. The last hour or day you will spend to complete something that is unnecessary. Just because you started it can be much better spent on more worthwhile activities.

Get it While it is Hot

Developing a system, processing thoughts, scheduling activities and managing your time in accordance with your own personal compass is great, but never let your system work against you. If something small enough comes across your table. Then get it while it's hot. If you know something is going to take you only two minutes or so, then do not spend a minute on it just to put it down and come back to it during the scheduled batching season. Remember that there is a cumulative effect and that if you ignore this effect, it can cost you dearly over the long term. Worst of all, you will not even notice it. Let's imagine that you are at the end of a highly productive Pobo email run and an e-mail comes in just as you're about to close your mail manager.

You spend a minute reading the contents of the email and realize it's only going to take you about three minutes to answer the mail, then get it while it's hot. This is much more productive than revisiting the mail later, having to reorganize your mind and then formulate your response. I do this with most small activities that come across my desk, whether it's small expense approval's leave approval or answering emails, Of course, only when my mail manager is actually open. There are times when it is more productive to handle something small than to write it in your notebook and revisit it later.

This little way of life is equally applicable to the small tasks at home as well. Instead of throwing your clothes on the floor in the bathroom and later having to come back around to pick everything up and go put it in the laundry basket, just throw it in the laundry basket from the start. Make your bed the moment you wake up, rather than having to come back to your room before you leave for work to make your bed, get into the habit of handling the small but unavoidable minutiae as and when they occur.

Capitalize on Your Commute

I used to hate my commute, 45 to 60 absolutely useless minutes in the car in the morning and the afternoon between home and the office. I would listen to news bulletins and drown in the frustration caused by all the other idiots on the road. The news made me negative. Other people who can't drive raised my blood pressure. And the idea that I was stuck wasting a good hour, being able to do absolutely nothing, really set the stage for an irritable guy during the first two hours of my day at work. Then I realized something. There's no reason why I should waste this time. And I began to dedicate my commute time to personal development. Thank you, 21st century. I started getting audio books and listening to interesting podcasts.

And before I knew it, I was actually looking forward to the commute. In fact, as part of my vehicle insurance package, I have an app that rates my driving safety and gives me reward points for driving safer. Since I started using my commute time more productively, I've become a much more placid and safe driver. And I do not pitch up at work just below my boiling point. And I'm learning much more than I would find the time to between work, my marriage and my two toddlers. The chapter learned to capitalize on your commute or any other unproductive time you stuck spending daily. There's no reason why you cannot get the most out of that time as well.

Win Your Day When You Start Your Day

There is one last thing that I didn't really get into as part of the main body of the Book, and that is a killer morning routine. I spoke about the importance of self-management when attempting effective time management. And I discussed the value of self-improvement. Now I want to try and convince you to incorporate your physiological and psychological well-being practices into your morning routine. Take the first 60 to 90 minutes of your day and devoted solely to yourself. And by that, I do not mean spending leisurely drinking coffee and using an hour to slowly get ready so you can start your high paced day slowly. I mean, devote the first 60 to 90 minutes of your day to improving yourself and bullying that machine that you are going to use to pilot through the rest of your day, week and year, all the way to your ultimate goals. Wake up between five and six a.m.

immediately. Drink a glass of water. Spend 10 to 15 minutes meditating. Go for a 20 to 30 minute run. Take a cold shower. Get dressed and spend a few minutes actively thinking about what you are grateful for. And conditioning your brain for a positive and productive day. This is an extremely powerful tool. But I did not include it in the main body of the Book, because I make a habit to only preach what I practice. My two and four year old kids currently take up the bulk of my mornings. And I have made a conscious decision to keep it that way for now. Neither of them can really get themselves ready for the day at daycare. And I like spending the first and last moments of their days with them.

My wife also has to leave home at six thirty in order to be at work on time. Our routines are thus a bit different than the one I just described a minute ago. We wake at around five forty five a.m.. My wife then starts to get herself ready for work, and I go, wake up the kids, dress them, brush their teeth, give them their vitamins and make sure they are ready for their day when they leave the house at six thirty with their mom. I go back, tidy up their rooms and make their beds at around six forty five. I usually go for a 30 minute high intensity cardio workout, usually just some high baserunning, after which I take a five minute ice cold shower. Summer or winter, I then get dressed and leave for work at around seven 30, listening to an audiobook or a podcast on my way to work.

I leave my meditation for a few minutes before I go to bed, simply because I don't really have the time to do it with clarity or a clear mind in the mornings. There may come a time in my life when my kids are a bit older that I may just adjust my morning routine to be a little bit more self-improvement centric. But for now, I like being the first and last contact at the start and end of my kids' day. I do, however, strongly believe and advocate for a powerful morning routine, supporting research for its merits, or just too vast and abundant for it not to be true. You can structure your routine any way you prefer. Just make sure you spend devoted time on self-improvement and conditioning. There are several books on the topic, and you will be hard pressed to find any of the famously successful people out there who do not take advantage of their early mornings and one way or another.

Recruitment And Selection

This chapter introduces the reader to recruitment and selection, the first chapter focuses on recruitment. We look at the definition of recruitment and describe recruitment, planning and the development of a recruitment strategy. In developing a recruitment strategy, it is necessary to determine who will do the recruiting, what kind of recruiting will be used, where will be done, and what sources and methods of recruitment will be used. The chapter then proceeds to the actual recruitment process, preliminary screening and evaluation of the recruitment efforts.

The second chapter focuses on a selection of staff. We define selection and describe the factors that should be considered before making selection decisions. When we look at the selection procedure, including the preliminary screening interview, completion of the applicant, blank psychometric tests, the selection interview, reference checks and physical examinations and requirements for selection predictors. We describe the factors that should be considered when rejecting applications and auditing the selection process. Learning outcomes, when you have completed this chapter, you should be able to, one, define recruitment and describe recruitment planning. To develop a recruitment strategy by considering the type of recruiters.

Needed kind of recruitment place of recruitment and sources and methods of recruitment. Identify the factors that should be considered during the actual recruitment process. For the fine selection and motivation, while selection is important for organizations. Five describe the factors which affect selection decisions and explain the requirements for selection predictors. Six evaluate the suitability of different selection predictors for different jobs. Seven discuss the considerations when applicants are rejected and develop a strategy to audit the selection process. Recruitment definition of recruitment. Recruitment is defined as a process of seeking and attracting suitable candidates from within the organization or from outside the organization for job vacancies that exist.

Suitable candidates means those who possess the required characteristics that will enable them to perform satisfactorily in the specific job. Recruitment, planning. Before any recruitment can be done, an organization needs to decide what the nature and number of job vacancies are. This information comes from human resource planning and job analysis in recruitment planning. That information is used to decide on the number and characteristics of potential candidates that need to be attracted. Organizations try to recruit more candidates than the number they wish to employ. Some candidates will most probably be overqualified for the specific position, while some might not really be interested in obtaining a position.

An organization needs to keep a balance between setting recruitment standards that are too high or too low. When an organization is operating in a so-called tight labor market where there are few candidates for the number of job openings, it may be tempted to lower standards regarding the candidate's qualifications. This might lead to other undesirable outcomes.

An organization might decide to retain high standards and to spend much time and money to attract suitable candidates. It seems that when organizations retain higher standards, fewer candidates apply for jobs, but then these candidates are also better qualified.

From past experience, organizations usually know how many potential candidates they need to reach through their recruitment efforts in order to have a sufficient number of applicants from which to choose. The number will most probably vary with the type of vacancy or job. The type of recruitment source and the recruitment method will also have to be taken into consideration when deciding on a number of candidates that have to be reached. Developing a recruitment strategy. When developing a recruitment strategy, an organization must answer the following questions.

Who will be doing the recruiting and how should they be prepared? What kind of recording will be used? Where will the recruiting be done? What sources and methods of recruitment will be used? Recruiters and their preparation and characteristics. In most organizations, the human resource department is responsible for the coordination of the recruitment process. Because recruiters come into direct contact with possible candidates, it is of great importance that they should be knowledgeable about the organization in general and about the specific jobs that are vacant.

Often, recruiters are the main source of information that potential candidates make use of in deciding to apply for a position. The reason for this is that potential applicants know so little about the organization, they have to make use of the information supplied by recruiters when deciding to apply for a position. The ideal recruiter is someone who can make potential applicants enthusiastic about the organization. A recruiter should have very good interpersonal skills and should be able to supply realistic information to possible applicants. He or she should be a likable person, be enthusiastic and must show personal interest in applicants.

Kind of recruitment. Both positive and negative aspects about the organization and job should be provided to applicants when an organization, through its recruiting efforts, gives applicants both positive and negative information about the organization and job in a balanced and objective way. It is called realistic job previews. One of the main reasons for giving a realistic job preview is to reduce the reality, shock and disappointment when a newcomer eventually joins an organization and finds that his or her expectations are not being met and or that circumstances are quite different from those which were envisaged.

Unless the applicant has no other option than to take the job offered to him or her a realistic job, Previa gives the applicant the chance to opt out without losing face because the decision to opt out is based upon realistic information. It also seems that if an applicant in the face of a realistic job, Prevue, still decides to join an organization, such a person will most probably be a more committed employee. Place of recruitment. Organizations tend to recruit managerial and professional employees on a countrywide or a regional basis, technical employees and artisans on a regional or a local basis, and clerical and manual workers on a local basis.

Generally speaking, organizations make use of past experience to decide where to concentrate their recruitment efforts and to get the best return on the money invested in recruitment. The bases of recruiting will also depend on the job seeking behavior of applicants. One aspect of job seeking behavior is, for instance, the distance of personal travel, looking for a job. Another aspect might be the media a potential candidate might use when searching for a job. The state of the labor market will also play a role if, for instance, there are very few qualified clerical workers available locally and the organization will concentrate its recruitment efforts on a regional basis.

Sources and methods of recruitment. Sources referred to the segments of the labor market where applicants can be found, such as schools, colleges, universities, other organizations and sources of unemployed people. Methods refer to the specific ways of obtaining applicants. Here, one can think of something like direct applications or so-called write ins or walk ins. Referrals by present employees, advertising using different media, private and public employment agencies and so-called executive search agencies and firms. It seems safe to say that sources do influence the methods used.

Internal recruitment. Internal recruitment has various advantages, a, most people at one time or another expect to be appointed to some higher position, having a greater status and paying a higher salary. If an organization appoints from within, it can lead to an increase in the morale of employees because their expectations are being met. B, it is possible to more accurately assess the knowledge, skill and personality characteristics of an organization's present employees than those of outside applicants who have to go through a selection process. See, the recruitment and selection process is simplified because with a few exceptions, candidates from outside sources are only needed for entry level jobs.

The career development of employees can be planned far more systematically and suitable career paths for them to follow can be more easily identified. E, the candidates already know how the organization operates. F The investment already made in present employees is continued. Recruiting and subsequent appointing from within also has some disadvantages, A, it leads to inbreeding that can prevent the development of new ideas and much needed creativity be an organization needs to have very good training programs in place through which the knowledge and skills of employees can be upgraded in order for them to be promoted to the vacant positions.

See if an organization wants to appoint from within. It needs to ensure that when candidates are first employed, they have the potential to be promoted, otherwise people might be promoted to a point where they are unable to carry out the duties of the job successfully. This might lead to infighting amongst colleagues, something that does the morale of employees no good. There are different internal recruitment methods that an organization can use. An informal search for a suitable candidate can be conducted.

This method is not recommended because it does not give everybody that might be interested or qualified a fair chance to apply for the specific job. A system of job posting and job building can be used for job postings simply means that vacancies are advertised internally in such a way that everyone that is eligible is able to take notice of the vacancy. When vacancies occur, the human resource information system can also be searched, such a system contains up to date information on each employee skills, abilities and personal characteristics.

Ben, Vacances do a cure used will also have to be made of the human resource plan. If career paths are in place for employees, it will also be clear which employees could be promoted to the vacant positions. External recruitment and organization makes use of a number of different recruitment methods to attract suitable candidates from outside the organization, it might be cheaper to hire certain categories of employees from outside than to train present employees.

The pool from which one can select is much greater, and people appointed from outside bring in new ideas. On the negative side, recruiting from outside sources might be quite costly, candidates from outside sources need more time to become oriented and adjusted to their new surroundings. Resentment can also develop in present employees when candidates from outside rather than themselves are appointed. The following external recruitment methods can be used. Advertisements, many organizations make use of advertisements in newspapers, magazines and professional journals and periodicals and over the radio and television to attract suitable candidates.

Reach The Right Audience

When recruitment advertisements are used, the following goals should be kept in mind first to reach the right audience target population and second, to attract sufficient suitable candidates and as few unqualified candidates as possible. This means that one has to understand the characteristics of the target population and what motivates them to apply for a vacancy. If one receives too many applications for a specific vacancy, then it shows that there is something wrong with the communication process. An effective recruitment advertisement appears to require the following conditions, A, it should be based on a thorough job description and must provide details about the job and about the job specification be in order to ensure that a realistic job preview is given.

It is important that the necessary unfavorable information about the job is also provided. C One should be specific in describing tasks and the remuneration package. D The facts should be presented in a positive way. Private employment agencies. These agencies have information on a large number of possible candidates on a computer, which can be matched against the job specifications of vacant jobs. If they do not have suitable candidates on file or on computer, they do the necessary advertising to attract the required candidates. A private employment agency is able to do a lot of the administrative work associated with recruitment. But they tend to charge large fees for their services.

Walk ins or write ins? This simply means that sometimes applicants go right into the organization to apply for jobs, even though no such jobs have been advertised. Sometimes applicants come in person to apply for jobs which have not been advertised. Referrals by employees. It often happens that the information that a vacancy exists is passed along by means of word of mouth among colleagues and their friends. The advantage of this recruitment method is that it is very time and cost effective. Unfortunately, it might lead to inbreeding and the forming of cliques.

Educational institutions. Organizations can only let reporters visit different educational institutions to recruit suitable candidates. Sometimes an organization is looking for candidates who possess specific scholastic, academic or professional qualifications. In order to reach these candidates, it is important for organizations to build up relationships with these educational institutions who will be more than willing to supply information on suitable candidates. Executive search firms. The US concentrates on the recruiting of middle and top managers in order for them to attract suitable candidates, these executive search firms take much care to ensure that the job specifications are clearly stated. Miguel and top managers recruited by means of this method are often drawn away from other organizations.

That is why this method of recruiting is often called head hunting. It is nothing out of the ordinary for them to ask a fee that amounts to one third of a successful candidate's annual salary. Other methods. There are a variety of other methods an organization can use to recruit suitable candidates, an organization may make use of direct mail recruiting by obtaining mailing lists from different professional bodies or societies and by sending the specific advertisements to all the people on these mailing lists. The recruiters may set up stands at job fairs or career exhibitions. See, many organizations also make use of the services of temporary help agencies. The actual recruitment process.

Once an organization has decided on a recruitment plan and their recruitment strategy, the following two broad steps have to be carried out. The potential sources of recruitment must be activated and the sales message must be communicated to qualified applicants. Activating the sources of recruitment. No recruitment is done before a request has been received from line management that a vacancy has occurred or is about to occur. Handyman and I'll point out that the recruitment process at this point in time can become an administrative and logistic nightmare for an organization because the following tasks have to be performed.

Preliminary screening of applicants has to be done to eliminate those candidates who are clearly unsuitable. Candidates have to be transported to the organization and will have to be housed for the duration of the selection process. Line managers must be ready to interview candidates. Candidates who have been unsuccessful must be notified to that effect. Formal employment offers must be sent to successful candidates. The acceptance or rejection of such offers must be processed. A well functioning record system which can be utilized at any moment to check what progress has been made in the recruitment process needs to be in place. Communicating the sales message to potential applicants.

And organizations should not oversell themselves to potential candidates. The organization should take note of the factors that influence a person's decision to apply for a job and to join an organization. It appears that the message and the medium through which it is communicated play a significant role in this regard. The message. A potential candidate is likely to apply for a job and to keep on working at the job if there is something in the remuneration package that attracts him or her. This has implications for the nature of the message that has to be communicated to the potential applicant.

Although there is no clear cut answer as to what should be included in this message, the following can be used as pointers. A salary and the nature of the work play a role in most candidates' decision to apply for a job. Be the geographical area in which the organization is located and the possibilities for advancement are important for people who apply for managerial or professional positions. See, job security is an important factor for unskilled or lower skilled workers. De. Working conditions, hours of work and the nature of supervisors and co-workers are often no great concern when applying for a job. The media.

The effectiveness of a recruitment message also largely depends on the medium through which the message is delivered. It seems that this credibility or believability of the medium plays an important role in getting the message across. Credibility of media is based on trust, perceived expertise and personal liking.

Therefore, media such as personnel agencies and recruitment advertisements have the least credibility, while the smaller and more intensive media such as friends and personal contacts, have the most credibility. Preliminary screening. There are several ways to go about doing preliminary screening, it might consist of doing a quick check on the application blanks that were returned by applicants.

One can also do a check on curriculum vitae and testimonials that were sent in by applicants. It might even consist of doing some reference, checking on applicants. In the case of walk-ins, the screening might consist of an interview with the applicant. Evaluation of recruitment. Several methods can be used to evaluate the recruitment effort of an organization, for instance, the outcomes of the recruitment effort could be studied. The following questions should be answered A, have all the vacancies been felt? B, what is the nature of the work, performance and labor turnover of applicants that have been accepted? See, what is the average cost incurred for every candidate that has been appointed? Is this cost in accordance with that? What has been planned for? Did everything in the recruitment process go according to plan? These are the type of questions you usually ask when doing a utility analysis of the recruitment effort.

A utility analysis of the different recruitment methods or media that were used can be done to get an indication of the relative costs and benefits of the different methods or media. Selection. Definition of selection. Selection involves the sorting out of applicants for a vacant job and the elimination of those applicants who do not fit the requirements of the job and or the organization. The content of different jobs differs, as do the abilities and skills required. For example, the abilities and skills that are required of a telephone operator differ from those required of the manager of a retail store. Applicants also differ regarding their abilities, aptitudes, skills, experience, age and education. Therefore, the objective of selection is to assess which applicant will best fit a specific job. The importance of selection.

Selection is a major expense for organizations, a lot of money is spent on recruitment, selection and training. In addition to these costs, there is the cost incurred by the new employees inability to meet performance requirements while learning the job. Often it takes a year before the employee actually deserves the salary for the position. The costs are even greater if the wrong person is hired. Despite the high costs of selection, research has shown conclusively that good selection pays off. Sometimes good selection methods are expensive to develop and refine, which can discourage organizations from investing in them. Selection, however, affects the quality of personnel and their test performance.

Training will also be more successful if you select the right quality people. Poor selection causes a poor fit between the job and the individual, which contributes to job dissatisfaction, poor performance and high labor turnover. Factors that influence the selection decision. There are three factors that may influence the selection decision, the job description and job specification. The organization and the social environment and the success of Hurdle or the multiple correlation approach. Job description and job specifications. If a selection program is to be successful, the employee characteristics stated in the job specification must accurately summarize what is necessary for effective performance on the job.

An accurate list of characteristics can only be generated after the organization has conducted a thorough job analysis. Job specifications, which are important for selection purposes, include education and training, experience, physical characteristics and personal characteristics and competencies. Organization and social environment. The organization Social Environment refers to the values of the organization, the way things are done, social cliques, openness to new employees and the personality of the manager. The object of selection will be to assess whether the applicant would adapt to these values and conditions, a match between the values of the employee and those of the organization contributes to his or her commitment.

This Election Approach

Three approaches, the success of hurdles approach, the compensatory approach and the combined approach can be used during selection. The success of hurdles approach. Using the success of Hertel approach, the candidate must fit the requirement of each step in the selection process. For example, the application for psychometric testing or medical examination to be considered for appointment. This approach saves time and money because it prevents unsuitable applicants going through the whole selection process. The compensatory approach. The compensatory approach allows very high performance on one selection procedure to compensate for low performance on another.

The combined approach. It is possible to combine successive hurdles and the compensatory approach. In this case, the abilities and motivation that are critical for success are first assessed. If the applicant does not fit these requirements, his or her application is rejected, if he or she fits the critical requirements, you or she goes through the whole selection process and then the selection decision is made. Selection procedure. A systematic selection procedure must be followed to make selection decisions. Selection procedures refer to procedures or actions that can be used to acquire and integrate information to make a recommendation and or final human resource decision. The assumption of a selection procedure is that the procedures used predict an important and relevant behavioral requirement or job performance.

This election procedure is given in figure eight point one. The procedure may be adapted depending on the job requirements. If physical requirements, for example, eyesight, fitness and hearing are important requirements, then the medical examination may take place earlier. Another important consideration is that the application form and psychometric tests must be administered prior to the selection interview to verify the results obtained during the interview. The next chapter focuses on the predictors that can be used as part of the selection procedure. Figure eight point one, the selection procedure. Application form to preliminary interview to reference check.

To psychometric testing, to medical examination, to selection interview by a psychologist, to selection interview by line manager. Then finally, the selection decision. Requirements for selection predictors. Personnel selection is based on individual differences between people, the work performance of different individuals also differs from stress, and the importance of individual differences in the selection of the right person for the right job. Before its election predictor is used, it must be valid, reliable and fair. Validity. The term validity refers to how well a measure assesses the attribute it is being used to assess. An intelligence test is valid if it measures intelligence as it is defined.

The validity of a predictor is not absolute, but is relative to its intended use, it is valid as long as it successfully measures the attribute that the user intends it to measure. In other words, a measure that is valid for one purpose may not be valid for another. And aptitude tests that are used for the selection of university students may not be valid for the selection of managers. The term validation refers to the process of assessing the validity of a measure. Validation indicates whether it is justifiable to make a particular interference from a score obtained on the predictor. Invalidity coefficient is a correlation coefficient between a predictor measure, for example, a psychometric test and a criterion measure, for example, work performance.

Applied to the same group of individuals. The correlation coefficient expresses the degree to which two sets of numbers are in agreement or correlated with each other. The following types of validity, you're distinguished. Criterion related validity. Criterion related validity measure scores, what a predictor, which is usually a selection device. It also measures scores on a criterion or a set of criteria. Which is usually job behavior, such as performance, absenteeism and training success. A predictor score and criterion score are obtained for each person in the sample, and the statistical relationship between the two sets of scores is computed.

Predictors and validation are usually chosen because they're similar to the actual selection techniques the organization is considering. A good predictor distinguishes applicants from each other and does it reliably good criteria should be a affected by individuals not determined largely by others or by technology, be relevant to the goals of key constituents in the organization, see measurable at reasonable cost with adequate quality and in practical ways, the affected by the individual differences reflected in the predictors and e remain stable over time. Sales performance might seem a complete criterion for the validation of a selection battery for sales personnel. However, sales may be contaminated by unrelated factors such as the territory assigned to individuals.

Sales performance may also be deficient by failing to reflect important factors such as working as part of a team and completing paperwork. Two types of criterion related validity, concurrent validity and predictive validity can be computed. Focus, eight point one types of criterion related validity. Concurrent validity. In the case of concurrent validity, the predictor scores, such as scores on IQ tests of current employees, are correlated with their job performance, such as quantity and quality of work. The predictor and criteria and data are gathered at the same time, which is why it's called concurrent validity. The correlation coefficient between the predictor and criterion is called the concurrent validity of the predictor.

In this case, the IQ test. Organizations use this method because time and cost considerations make it impossible to determine the predictive validity of a predictor. The disadvantage of the concurrent validity design is that poor performers are not included in the study and that employees may perform better on the predictor because of their experience. Predictive validity. Predictive validity indicates if a predictor such as an IQ test can be used to predict future behavior. Predictor scores are gathered from a sample of applicants, not current employees, next, selection decisions are made regarding these applicants without considering their scores on the predictor.

The applicants are selected by using methods used in the past, excluding the predictor that you want to validate. Criterion scores such as quality and quantity of work ratings of supervisors are gathered after the employees have been working for a while. For example, six months after that, the correlation between the predictor and criterion is calculated. Predictive validity is indicated if the employee who scored high on the predictor performs well on the job. This method eliminates the disadvantages of the concurrent validity design, which requires more time and administration. The results are also not immediately available. Content validity.

A predictor has content validity if its items are representative of important aspects of a dimension or the job. For example, are the items of an IQ test representative of what can be defined as intelligence, does the application form include questions about the most important aspects of the applicant in relation to the job? Constructability: a predictor such as an intelligence test has constructability if it correlates with a specific construction, such as intelligence. It takes time to assess the construct validity of a test, because the relationship between a predictor and other measuring instruments must be determined. Face validity. Face validity is a non-statistical type of validity, which indicates what the test measures on face value.

It refers to the judgment of the validity of a predictor by the person on whom it is administered. An engineer who was tested may easily assess the material used in the predictor and identify irrelevant aspects. Hi, face validity is needed to create a positive attitude towards the predictor. Reliability. The reliability of a predictor refers to the consistency of performance of the same individual on the predictor at different times. For example, if you test the person's blood pressure with the device today and you test it again after two weeks, the device must give the same results. If there was no change in the person's blood pressure.

I predict you must be reliable. The DiCicco procedures are used to obtain a numerical estimate of a measured reliability. The most common numerical estimate is called a reliability coefficient. Basically, the reliability coefficient measures the extent of agreement among two or more applications of the same measurement device to the same group of individuals. To be reliable, the test must have a reliability coefficient higher than zero point nine five. The reliability of a measurement device or predictor is not a guarantee of its validity. Reliability only indicates the consistency of measurement and not the extent to which it measures what it is supposed to measure. However, a predictor cannot be valid if it's unreliable.

Reliability of a predictor is essential, but not adequate for its validity. The reliability of a predictor must be indicated in its manual. Different types of reliability are defined in focus box eight point two. Focus, eight point two. Types of reliability. Test retest reliability indicates the relationship between scores of the same people on the same predictor on different occasions. Parallel forms, reliability in the case, the correlation between predictor scores of the same people in equivalent forms of the same test on different occasions. Greater reliability is assessed by calculating the correlation between the ratings of answers on a predictor by different assessors.

Projective Personality Tests

Such as in projective personality tests. This type of reliability gives an indication of the objectivity of scoring procedures. Internal consistency, reliability indicates the homogeneity of the items of the predictor. Although items are interdependent, they must focus on the same content area. Hi, internal consistency is the result of high correlation coefficients between items and equal difficulty of items. Varanus. Fairness is a perceptual variable along which people will differ. There are several variables that affect perceptions of fairness and some potential outcomes associated with these perceptions. The processes and procedures used.

A selection procedure will be perceived as fair when a subjective decision making by the employer is minimized by the selection process being consistent across applicants. For example, interview questions should be the same for males and females. See, the selection process is not subject to manipulation. Applicants should be examined against a common set of standards. The selection process is developed and managed by professionals, professionals often rely on sets of selection standards that help to ensure fairness. E the organization maintains the confidentiality of data supplied by the candidate. F The review of applicant information is made by several individuals who represent different perspectives and constituents.

The nature of information using variables that are explicitly illegal would be perceived as unfair by most candidates. Rivals based on merit, such as talent, abilities, experience, are considered more fair than variables that are not such as family connection or political loyalty. Variables that are job related are considered more fair than variables that are not variables that seem related to the job content validity show empirical relationships to important aspects of the job, empirical validity. Or reflect central psychological constructs important to the job construct validity are perceived as more fair than variables that bear no direct relationship to the job.

Information that invades the privacy of a candidate will be considered less fair than information that does not. The use of selection instruments that probe candidates' personal lives, explore sexual habits or invade these emotional components believed to be private may be perceived as unfair. The relative outcomes achieved. Perceptions of fairness have to do with whether the right number of disadvantaged people, for example, blacks, women were selected compared to a majority group, usually white males. If these people are disadvantaged in the selection process, the organization must show the job relatedness of the selection device. The component of selection fairness emphasizes the outcomes.

Of prediction and test use instead of the selection procedures and information used. Different constituents. Different constituents may have different perceptions of fairness, even when the procedures used, the information gathered and the relative outcomes achieved are kept constant. What might be perceived as fair by one constituent might not be perceived as fair by another. These perceptions will differ according to whether the applicant was hired or not. Situational factors, perceptions of selection, fairness might depend on situational factors, for instance, whether an organization has a history of hiring minorities and whether the organization has enjoyed high profits and could therefore afford to hire protected group members. Types of selection predictors.

The most important selection predictors will be discussed next. The application form. The application form consists of questions designed to provide information on the general suitability of applicants for jobs they're seeking. The questions address the applicant's educational background, previous job experience, physical health and other areas that may be useful in judging a candidate's ability to perform a job. The application form serves as a means for deciding if the applicant meets the minimum requirements of a position and assessing the candidate's strengths and weaknesses. It serves as a basis for the selection interview and supplies information for human resource information systems.

A problem with application forms is the possibility that the applicant will provide inaccurate information when people are competing for a job, they may distort information that they give in order to look good. Distortion can range from inflation of school and university grades to outright lies involving types of jobs held by companies for whom they worked or educational degrees earned. This happens especially when it is difficult, timely and costly to verify the information. If the candidate supplies false or misleading information, the organization may terminate his or her application.

Psychometric testing. A psychometric test is a systematic, standardized and objective procedure to observe a sample of an individual's behavior and to quantify it on a scale. A score which indicates the individual score on a continuum is awarded on the basis of his or her performance on the test. Each item is an observation of the individual's behavior, the test of items is a representative sample of the total spectrum of the concept measured. For example, a test that measures the ability to solve arithmetic problems represents a sample of a universe of earth medical problems.

It measures a representative sample of an individual's or athletic ability. Psychometric tests are subject to mistakes because a sample of observations which may not be representative of the universe is used. Psychometric tests can be classified in different ways, namely administrative considerations and test content. The following classification of psychometric tests can be made on the basis of administrative considerations. Speed tests versus power tests. Speed tests usually have demanding time limits. The amount of work completed per time unit is manifested in the scores on these tests. Speed tests are used when individuals must solve problems in the short time span.

Speed is also a factor in certain skills, for example, typing. Howard tests have no time limits. The individual gets sufficient time to complete the test, and if a time limit is used, it is usually for the convenience of the tester. Group tests versus individual tests. Group tests are administered at the same time on a group of people. These tests are especially used for selection and placement purposes because they allow many candidates to be tested on one day. Individual tests are administered on an individual basis and are expensive. Individual tests are used for high level selection and when interpersonal rapport with the candidate is important.

Paper and pencil tests versus performance tests. Paper and pencil tests are used for selection purposes. The individual scores on these tests are not related to the manipulation of physical objects or equipment. Examples of these tests include the verbal comprehension test and the mechanical insight test. These tests are increasingly being replaced by computers. Performance tests require that the individual respond by manipulating specific physical objects or equipment. The individual scores on a performance test are related to the quantity and quality of manipulation of the object or equipment, such as a practical driving test. Aptitude versus proficiency test. An aptitude test measures an individual's future potential for a specific activity.

The objective of a proficiency test is to assess the applicant's level of proficiency at the time of the testing, for example, a knowledge test. The following classification of psychometric tests can be made on the basis of test content. Ability tests. Ability tests measure individual characteristics that can lead to learning specific skills. It indicates which tests the individual will be able to perform if he or she receives the necessary training and which tests he or she is able to perform currently. Ability tests include cognitive tests, mechanical and spatial tests, perceptual accuracy tests, motor tests and physical tests. Focus, eight point three types of ability tests.

Cognitive tests include intelligent tests and aptitude tests. Intelligence tests measure abilities that can be used in different situations and jobs. Most items measure some combination of vocabulary, symbol, manipulation, mathematics, reading comprehension and reasoning. Aptitude tests measure abilities that are more situation than job specific, such as verbal comprehension, word fluency, general reasoning, perceptual speed and memory. In perceptual accuracy tests, which are especially important in clerical jobs, it is expected from the individual to compare a standard stimulus with a test stimulus to determine the differences. Mechanical tests measured the individual's comprehension of mechanical principles.

Spatial tests measured the ability to manage concrete material through visualization. That is the ability to determine the appearance of an object if it is rotated. Motor tests measure physical abilities, for example, finger dexterity, speed of our movement, arm hand stability, finger speed and reaction time. Physical tests include fitness tests, cardiovascular power, muscle power and physical ability for jobs that are physically demanding. Personality tests. Personality tests include objective tests and projective tests. Objective tests, personality questionnaires are paper and pencil tests with a clear stimulus, such as statements regarding preferences for different lifestyles and clear responses that may be selected.

Personality questionnaires. Our concern with measures of emotional adjustment and tendencies towards extroversion or introversion. The five factor model of personality enjoys considerable support in personnel selection. Interest questionnaires. Interest questionnaires can be used to determine likes and dislikes for various activities. Some people would rather work indoors than outdoors. Some like to deal with people. Others prefer working with machinery. Some clear responsibility, others strive to avoid it by matching interests and vocations, it is quite apparent that job satisfaction and motivation at least can be increased. As another questionnaire, the respondents can fake their results if motivated to do so.

Performance Results

For example, tests or samples of tasks that are performed in a specific job. The assumption of these tests is that performance results acquired from realistic simulations of the job. Are the best predictor of work performance. Most studies in which work samples were used report validity coefficients higher than zero point five zero. Research methods, eight point one. Validity of selection predictors. Research shows that ability tests are supported by favorable validity data. Ability tests, including intelligence and aptitude tests, are valid predictors of work, performance and success in training programs in various jobs and occupations. Personality tests and interest questionnaires have lower validity for selection purposes.

Few studies indicated significant correlation coefficients between. Personality tests and interest questionnaires and job performance. However, it seems that these tests are very useful for the selection of management and sales personnel. References. References can be used as a predictor for selection purposes because it is not as expensive and time consuming as other methods. It is based on the assumption that past behavior is a good predictor of future behavior. The following references can supply information about applicants. Educational institutions. Schools, colleges and universities can be visited or contacted to inquire about the candidates, Mark's position in the class, extracurricular activities, motivation and emotional adaptability. Previous employers.

Previous employers can supply information about the applicant's quality and quantity of work, participation, personality characteristics, initiative and interpersonal relationships. The accuracy of the information supplied by the candidate can be verified, as well as jobs held, salary and reason for quitting. Testimonials, the candidate can be asked to nominate friends as a reference. Friends are usually not able to assess a candidate's job behavior. Few validation studies were done on references and testimonials, which makes it difficult to judge the validity thereof. These reports are usually favorable and do not discriminate between good and poor candidates.

The problem may be overcome by informing the suppliers of the reports about the information needed and by giving feedback to them regarding the usefulness of their information. Physical examinations. Some organizations require that those most likely to be selected for a position, complete a medical questionnaire or take a physical examination. These reasons for such a requirement include a case of later workers compensation claims. Physical condition at the time of the hiring should be known. B, it is important to prevent the hiring of those with serious communicable diseases. This is especially so in hospitals, but it applies to other organizations as well.

See, it may be necessary to determine whether the applicant is physically capable of performing the job under question. These purposes can be served by the completion of a medical questionnaire, a physical examination or a work's physiology analysis. The last of these is neither a physical examination nor a psychomotor test. It is used for the selection of manual workers who will be doing hard labor. The purpose of work physiology analysis is to determine by physiological indexes. Heartbeat and oxygen consumption, the true fatigue endangered by the work. Physical examinations have not been shown to be very reliable as a predictor of future medical problems. This is at least partially due to the state of the art of medicine.

Different physicians emphasize different factors in the exam based on their training and specialties. There is evidence that correlating the presence of certain past medical problems, as learned from a medical questionnaire, can be as reliable as a physical examination performed by a physician and probably less costly. Interviews. Interviewing is probably the most popular and most criticized method of employee selection. This popularity seems to prevail at all job levels from unskilled to executive. Despite its popularity, the interview has been criticized as unreliable and invalid.

The lack of reliability and validity raises potential legal hazards if an interview appears to discriminate unfairly, management may face an uphill battle in court because of the generally low validity of most interviewing approaches. Besides, the interview is often a subjective process that allows the intrusion of personal biases and this factor arouses the suspicion of the court. A selection interview can be defined as a conversation with three objectives, namely, A, to provide information about an applicant's suitability for a job and organization to the interviewer, be to provide information about the job and organization to the applicant and see to treat the applicant in such a way that a positive attitude towards the organization is maintained.

Interviews may be unreliable and invalid, partially because they are often done in a haphazard way. Therefore, specialists are urging employers to use structured rather than unstructured interviews. Focus, eight point four structured versus unstructured interviews. A structured interview is an interviewing method in which the content format and evaluation of the interview are specified in advance and followed by the interviewer. The structured interview is generally more reliable and valid than the unstructured interview, perhaps because more attention is paid. The purpose of the interview and more time is spent in planning it. An unstructured interview is an interviewing method in which the content format and evaluation of the interview are not specified in advance.

Unstructured interviews may lead to a hasty evaluation of the candidate. The advantage of the unstructured interview over the structured interview is that it yields more detailed information about the applicant's experiences, feelings and values. This format allows interviewers to consider factors and initiate discussions that they might not have planned in advance. The following recommendations can be made regarding selection interviews. Restrict the use of interviews to characteristics and behavior that interviewers can access more effectively. The interview is appropriate to measure personal relations characteristics such as sociability and verbal fluency and good citizenship characteristics such as dependability, consistency and stability.

A third characteristic job knowledge has also been evaluated in interviews, but other predictors may be more suitable for this purpose. Incorporate more structure in the interview format. The reason for structure is to ensure that the interviewer consistently gathers information about all relevant requirements from each applicant. Because the interviewer has information from each applicant on the same characteristics, it is easier to choose among the applicants. Use job related questions. The most useful questions provide direct, specific information about characteristics required on the job. Detailed questions about the applicant's participation in work, training or educational activities relevant to the job.

Make the scoring formal. The most commonly used formal systems require the interviewer to rate the interviewee on a series of characteristics. The rating scales have a number at each point, each with an objective, for example, not acceptable, marginal, minimal, good and superior or a brief description. Use a panel interview. In a panel interview, several interviewers meet as a group with the applicant; panel interviews are frequently used to hire technical or highly skilled personnel. Planning is essential to the success of the panel interview. One interviewer should be the chairperson and each interviewer should question the applicant and turn. There should be assigned areas where each interviewer to question and evaluations should be completed separately, but each interviewer. Train the interviewer.

The main skills of an interviewer include accurately receiving information, critically evaluating the information received and regulating his or her own behavior and asking questions.

Assessment centers. An assessment center is not a building or a place, an assessment center is defined as a multi method, multi trade and even multimedia technique. It is a series of individual and group exercises in which a number of candidates participate while being observed by several specially trained judges. Assessment centers are designed to provide a view of individuals performing critical work behaviors. The candidates are asked to complete a series of evaluative tests and exercises and to attend feedback sessions.

The popularity of the assessment center can be attributed to its capacity for increase in an organization's ability to select employees who will perform successfully in management positions. In the assessment centers, a wide array of methods, including several interviews, work samples and simulations and many kinds of paper and pencil tests of abilities and attitudes are used. Most assessment centers are similar in a number of areas. Groups of approximately 12 individuals are evaluated. Individual and group activities are observed and evaluated. Multiple methods of assessment are used, these include interviewing, objective testing, projective testing games, role plays and other methods.

Assessors doing the evaluation are usually a panel of line managers from the organization. They can, however, be consultants or outsiders trained to conduct assessment. Assessment centers are relevant to the job and have higher appeal because of this. As a result of candidates participating as part of a group and as individuals completing exercises, interviews and tests, the assessors have a large volume of data on each individual. Individuals are evaluated on a number of dimensions, such as organization and planning, ability, judgment, analysis, decisiveness, flexibility and resistance to stress. The Rainard judgment is consolidated and developed into a final report.

The Assessment Center Report

Each candidate's performance in the center can be described if the organization wants this type of report. Portions of the individual reports are fed back to each candidate, usually by one or more members of the assessment team. The assessment center report can be used to determine the suitability of individuals for particular positions. The promote ability of individuals, individuals functioning in a group and training and development needs of candidates. Research on assessment centers has indicated that they are a valid way to select. Managers. Assessment centers can predict future success with some accuracy.

The disadvantages of assessment centers are that they are a relatively expensive managerial selection technique. In some circumstances, less costly and complicated techniques may sometimes be just as effective. Making the final selection decision. The final step in the selection process is choosing one individual for the job. If there is more than one qualified person of value, judgment based on all of the information gathered in the previous steps must be made to select the best candidate. In many organizations, the human resource department handles the completion of application forms, testing, interviewing and reference checking and arranges physical examinations. The final selection decision is usually left to the manager of the department with the job opening. Rejecting applicants.

Interviewers being no different from other people in this respect, frequently find it difficult to inform an applicant directly to his or her face that he or she does not measure up to the organization's standards. A person may feel rejected when his or her application is rejected. If those responsible for making the employment decision are sure in their own minds that the applicant should not be hired, there is no justification to holding up vague hopes. If it is a well qualified individual, but there are no openings at present for his or her talents, it is expected that there will be openings in the near future. It makes sense to inform him or her.

The interviewer has the three fold objectives of maintaining the person's ego and self concept, maintaining goodwill towards the organization and definitely letting the applicant know that he or she has been rejected. There are a number of ways of communicating to the person that he or she is being rejected. If the applicant can clearly see that his or her vocational aptitudes and interests or wage level needs are totally incompatible with the situation, he or she may withdraw. If the individual possesses certain skills and abilities that might be appropriate in another job situation, he or she may be informed that while the pattern of his or her skills, interests and abilities is good or she does not match the particular job for which the organization is hiring.

If the person possesses all the required technical abilities but is rejected because of personality, this presents a difficult challenge to the interviewer. Says personality traits cannot be measured objectively. There is a danger of creating the feeling that the candidate is discriminated against if he or she is told that his or her personality is unsuitable. This situation demands real skill on the part of the interviewer to diplomatically convey the message that the interviewee is being rejected. At times, it is best to imply that the organization is going to pick just one or a very few out of a number of good candidates. The competitive situation will mean that just the top few will be hired. Auditing the selection effort.

In order to ensure that the selection process accomplishes the results expected, a comprehensive audit should be conducted. The following issues can be examined in such an audit. Does the selection program meet affirmative action standards? Is there a delay in filling job openings? What percentage of those who apply are hired? What percentage of those hired, resigned or discharged during the probation period? What is the cost of the selection per person hired? How well do the predictions derived from each of the selection techniques correlate with job performance? How well do those hired perform at the jobs? Has feedback been obtained from applicants regarding treatment received throughout the selection process? In the news, application eight one, removing bias from recruitment.

Public Service Review Home Office issued 15 Wednesday, twenty first of March, two thousand seven. Debbie, W-W that public service that sees the UK. Peter Thickett, Direction of Human Resources at Lothian and Borders police reports on how the Scottish police forces are initiating screening for racial biases when recruiting. Following the BBC, the secret policeman program in 2003, which revealed very serious issues concerning attitudes to race among police trainees at a non residential training center in. New. England, the Association of Chief Police Officers in Scotland, initiated a review of the recruitment and training processes for the country's eight police forces.

Following the reviews, which were thought to be robust, the eight Scottish police forces reported that they had over the years rejected a small number of applicants on the grounds of concerns about attitude to race. It was noted, however, that forces had not been keeping records of such rejections or at what stage in the process applicants were rejected. As all police recruits to Scottish forces attend the Scottish Police College actually, Alan, for lengthy residential training, SBC structures are able to observe changes in both work and social situations and to take action to tackle inappropriate language and behavior.

AC s then reviewed what other organizations had done to add screening to the selection processes, but discovered that little had been done and what had been done looked unreliable. MultiChoice questionnaires were thought to be untrustworthy and responses easily faked. Candidates could be expected to guess what the correct answer might be or to find ways of communicating the right answers to others through the Internet. For example, The association was looking for a tool to provide additional quality assurance as to the recruitment selection processes. In pursuit of improved consistency between forces, Scottish police forces have in recent years introduced a national application form and recruitment standards, including updated medical standards.

The ideal tool turned out to be a psychometric test being developed by a Glasgow based company, Human Factors Analyst Limited, whose approach had been developed from leading research in the rail and nuclear industries. A spouse has worked in close collaboration with each FHL to develop a tool that meets demanding technical requirements, but also makes sense to recruiters and police managers. Additionally, a CPA identified that Scottish police forces needed to assure potential black and minority ethnic recruits that we meant it when we said that police forces sought to exclude people with racist attitudes from engagement. And the association wanted to signal to all recruits what forces were aiming to achieve.

To deter bad candidates and encourage good ones. The Commission for Racial Equality C, r, e has stated that it believes that forces are making genuine and sincere efforts to recruit from minority communities, but that perception of the police as an employer in these communities needs to be changed. The test is not a pass or fail, it provides for interviewers to investigate further within the selection process and adds to all the other information collected about candidates from application form, familiarization evening's standard entrance tests, assessment centers, criminal record and intelligence vetting, and first and final interviews. AC powers and the Scottish Police Service make no apologies for the care with which police officers are selected and will continually seek to monitor results and improve the selection processes.

No selection process can guarantee 100 percent success, but AC powers and the Scottish Police Service will work robustly to minimize the risks. Summary. Recruitment has been defined as the process of attracting suitable candidates to apply for vacancies that exist in an organization. Recruitment forms a crucial part of the overall human resource provisioning or employment process. It is thus very important to carefully plan a recruitment process and the organization needs to decide whether it will primarily use inside or outside sources when doing recruiting. It is therefore also important to develop a recruitment strategy. When developing such a strategy, one has to look into the characteristics of recruiters, the kind of recruiting to be done, where recruiting will be done and what sources and methods of recruiting will be used.

The objective of selection is to obtain the employers who are most likely to meet the organization's standards of performance and who will be staffed and developed on the job. The following points were stressed. Selection is influenced by job and organization factors. Reasonable criteria for the choice must be set prior to prediction. The selection procedure includes the preliminary screening interview, completion of the applicant, blank psychometric tests, the selection interview, reference checks and physical examinations. The predictors used must be valid, reliable and fair. Using a greater number of accepted methods to gather data for selection decisions, increases the number of successful candidates elected.

Larger organizations are more likely to use sophisticated selection techniques. Even if the most able applicant is chosen, there is no guarantee of successful performance on the job. Key concepts and terms. Ability, test application form. Assessment center. Combined approach, compensatory approach.

Concurrent validity. Construct validity, content, validity. Criterion related validity, external recruitment, executive search firm. Face validity, fairness, interest questionnaire, internal consistency, internal recruitment into greater reliability interview. Parallel forms, reliability, personality test, predictive validity, preliminary screening.

Private employment agency. Psychometric test, recruitment, recruitment, planning, recruitment, strategy, reference, reliability, selection, selection procedure, successive approach, test retest reliability. Utility analysis validity. Walk-ins work sample tests. Sample essay titles. Which factors should be taken into account when trying to give realistic job previews? What factors influence an organization's choice of selection methods? How can an organization improve the validity of its interviews? What is an assessment center? How will you develop an assessment center? What can be done to promote fair selection in organizations?

Induction, Training And Development In Organizations

This chapter introduces the reader to induction, training and development in organizations. The first chapter focuses on the definition of terms. The chapter then proceeds to introduce the introduction of new employees to an organization. We look at the objectives of induction, investigate who should be responsible for induction, focus on the content of an induction program, and describe how induction programs can be evaluated. The third chapter focuses on training and development of employees. We focus on the goals of training and the training cycle, such as needs assessment, the development and presentation of training programs and the evaluation of training programs.

Learning outcomes. When you've completed this chapter, you should be able to, one, define induction and training. To discuss the content of an induction program, we discussed the follow up and evaluation of an induction program. To discuss the goal and objectives of training by explaining the training cycle six, discuss the identification of training needs. Seven explain learning principles and evaluate different training methods. Eight distinguish between the four levels of evaluation of training programs. Induction. Definition of terms. Training is a process that involves the acquisition of knowledge, skills and attitudes to increase the performance of employees.

Training is directed at the improvement of skills, including motor skills, cognitive skills and interpersonal skills. Economic, social, technological and governmental changes influence the objectives and strategies of all organizations. Changes in these areas can make the skills learned today obsolete in the future. Organizational changes and expansion can also make it necessary for employees to update their skills and acquire new ones. A formal training program is an effort by the employer to provide opportunities for the employee to acquire job related knowledge, skills and attitudes. Learning is the act by which the individual acquires knowledge, skills and attitudes that result in relatively permanent changes in behavior.

Knowledge is divided into declarative and procedural knowledge. Declarative knowledge refers to factual information about a specific topic, what procedural knowledge refers to routines on how to do something? An individual should have declarative knowledge before he or she can have procedural knowledge. Any behavior that has been learned is a skill. Attitudes are evaluative tendencies towards an object. Training is often distinguished from education. Education has a broader scope. Education is considered to be formal education, law school, college or university, whereas training is vocationally oriented and of course, in a work organization.

Management development is a systematic program by which individuals gain and apply knowledge, skills, insights and attitudes to manage work organizations effectively. Briars and very defiant induction as the introduction of new employees to the organization, work unit and job. One finds that some writers talk about induction, while most others mention orientation. Induction includes relinquishing certain attitudes, values and behaviors as a new recruit learns the organization's goals, the means of obtaining those goals, basic job responsibilities, effective job behavior and workplace. Much of this is learned on the job from co-workers and work teams. Induction is geared towards the fitting end of the new employee with the way in which an organization operates.

It is a learning process which starts during recruitment and continues after the new employees are placed in the job. It is correctly regarded as forming part of the training and development process. Induction as a human resource management activity. The objectives of induction. Induction has three objectives first, learning job procedures, second, establishing relationships with co-workers, including subordinates and superiors. And fitting into the employer's way of doing things for which purpose, realistic job expectations and a positive attitude towards the employer are developed, and third, to give the employee a sense of belonging by showing him or her how the job fits into the overall organization. Induction has the following objectives.

It helps to create realistic employee expectations, especially in the case of new employees who have a long professional training period which provides much practical work experience. During their training period, people such as attorneys and general practitioners learned to a large extent what to expect in the actual work situation. It helps to make the new employee become productive sooner. This happens when a new employee is taught how the work is to be done, how the organization functions, and how he or she fits into the organization. It helps to reduce the fear, anxiety and insecurity experienced by the new employee. New employees are unsure whether they will succeed on the job.

A well organized induction program will tend to put these fears at rest. It helps to reduce the possibility that the new employee may leave soon after joining the organization. Staff turnover tends to be rather high during the first few months after new employees join an organization. If a new employee can see that he or she can make a positive contribution towards the activities of the organization, this tendency to leave will be reduced. It helps to create job satisfaction and a positive attitude towards the organization. If during the induction program, the new employee senses that the organization takes an interest in him or her as a human being.

Wants to make the job climate a pleasant one and that he or she is being treated with dignity, he or she will tend to develop a positive attitude towards the organization. It saves the time of superiors and coworkers because during a well planned and well executed induction program, the new employees know what is expected of him, her and how his or her tasks have to be carried out. If this happens, it means that there is very little need to correct mistakes later. Who is responsible for induction? The decision about who should be responsible for induction depends on the particular circumstances.

For instance, the size of the organization, the size of the human resource department, the role that a labor union and its officials play in the induction process and the general policy of the organization regarding induction. In bigger organizations, it appears to be a shared responsibility. In this case, the responsibility is shared between the human resource department and the managers or supervisors. The responsibility of the human resource department is for the general orientation of new employees. Well, a lot of the managers or supervisors may be termed the mentor and job orientation.

Beech points out that in some organizations, the human resource department exerts staff control over line supervisors by requiring them to fill out a checklist form to show which specific orientation tasks they have provided for each new employee. Dryer's and also referred to the so-called buddy system in which the job orientation is conducted by one of the new employees, fellow workers. The content of induction programs. The content of an induction program depends upon the particular circumstances. Besides providing your employees with a well-structured orientation program, it is also advisable to issue them with written material that they can always refer back to.

It is desirable for each new employee to receive an orientation kit or packet of information to supplement the verbal orientation program. This kid is normally prepared by the human resource department and can provide a wide variety of materials. Care should be taken in the design not only to ensure that essential information is provided, but also that too much information is not given. Some orientation materials that might be included in an orientation kit include the company organization chart and map of the company's facilities, a copy of the Policy and Procedures Handbook.

A list of holiday and fringe benefits. Pupusa, performance appraisal forms and procedures. Copies of other required forms such as expense reimbursement form. Emergency and accident prevention procedures, sample copy of company letter or magazine. Telephone numbers and locations of key company personnel. And copies of insurance plans. Many organizations require new employees to sign a form indicating that they have received and read the orientation kit. This is done to protect the organization if a grievance should arise and the employer should allege that he or she had not been aware of certain organizational policies and procedures.

Follow up and evaluation of induction programs. It is important to follow up any induction activities, it is of very little use if the human resources manager tells the new employee that he or she should drop by if any problems occur. The human resource department should have a scheduled follow up one month after the new employee has been placed. The supervisor or manager should also check how well the new employees are doing. The supervisor or manager should also answer any questions that the new employee has to ask about aspects that have arisen since he or she attended the orientation program. The Human Resource Department should also, on an annual basis, evaluate the total induction program.

This should be done to determine whether the program is meeting the needs of the organization as well as the needs of new employees. Data gathered during such an evaluation can be used to improve the program. Feedback from new employees can be used to evaluate the effectiveness of a program. Various methods can be used to obtain feedback, namely unsign questionnaires that are completed by all employees. Be in-depth interviews with randomly selected new employees. See group discussion sessions with new employees who have settled into their jobs. From the above mentioned feedback that is received, an organization can adapt its induction program.

An organization should make use of the suggestions that employees made during the feedback sessions. This is important because the induction process has a definitive impact on the performance of the new employee. Training. The goals of training. Training is only one component of the development process that includes all of the experiences that enhance and build employees employment related characteristics. The problem is, however, that a training program frequently occurs because a few people decide it is needed or because the latest fad can be sold to top management. They find the money to get it started and measure success by how many people participate. Effectiveness is seldom measured. The best companies integrate training within a systematic set of human resource activities, including selection rewards and job design.

Strategic Tool For Attaining The Goals

Training can be used as a strategic tool for attaining the goals of the organization and the employees. The link between training and strategic goals seems obvious, but it is often lost in the day to day struggle to implement programs and deal with crises. In that case, training becomes an activity rather than a strategy. Training as an activity is characterized by no client, no business need, no assessment of performance effectiveness, no effort to prepare the work environment to support training and no measurement of results. Training as a strategy is characterized by a partnership with the client linked to a business need assessment of performance effectiveness, preparation of the work environment to support training and measurement of results.

The reasons we're training can be summarized as follows: to give employees direction in their jobs and acquaint them with their working environment so that they can become productive quickly. To provide the human resources that are necessary for commerce and industry to be effective. To increase loyalty and increase the morale of employees. To improve the quality and quantity of an organization's output and to reduce costs. The training cycle. The training cycle consists of three phases. These phases include the following. Identification of training and development means. Training and development. Evaluating the training and development program.

Identification of training needs. Training must be directed towards the accomplishment of some organizational objectives, such as more efficient production methods, improved quality of products and services, or reduced operating costs. The organization should commit its resources only to those training activities that can best help in achieving its objectives. Needs assessment is a systematic analysis of the specific training activities required by jobholders and an organization to achieve the objectives of the job and the organization. The organizational needs assessment requires an examination of the long term and short term objectives of the organization.

The organization's financial, social, human resource growth and market objectives need to be matched with its human talent structure, climate and efficiency. The knowledge, skills and abilities needed to perform the job are carefully considered. What are the tasks, what skills are needed to perform well? What does performing well mean? Data from current employees, supervisors and experts need to be collected to complete this part of the needs assessment. The employee's needs must also be considered. Ask the employee what he or she needs to come to perform tasks. This will provide useful information.

Evaluate the employee's performance against a standard or the outputs of co-workers to help identify strengths, weaknesses and needs. Training can improve the individual's performance only when the employee does not have the knowledge and skills to do the job. The low performance is not due to a lack of practice and see, the low performance is not due to other causes. Wexler and Latham identified five methods that can be used to gather needs assessment information. Interviews, questionnaires, observation, focus groups and document examination. Focus, nine point one. Methods to assess training needs. Interviews. Interviews with employees can be conducted by human resource specialists or by external consultants.

The following question should be investigated. A lot of problems the employee experiences in the job. B, what knowledge and or skills does the employee need to improve performance on the job? See, what training does the employee feel is needed? If interviews are to provide useful information, employees must feel that their input will be valued and not be used against them. Questionnaires. Questionnaires can be used to assess training. This involves developing a list of skills required to perform a particular job effectively and asking employees to check those skills in which they believe they need training. Attitude surveys and customer service can also be used to determine training means. Observation.

A specialist can observe the behavior of employees in their jobs and translate these observations into training means. Focus groups. Focus groups are composed of employees from various departments and levels in the organization. Each group investigates the following questions with the help of a facilitator. What knowledge or skills will employees need in order for the organization to stay competitive over the next five years? B for problems, does the organization experience that can be solved through training? Document examination. Document examination is concerned with examining organizational records on absenteeism, turnover and accident rates to determine if problems exist and to determine if problems can be solved through training.

Performance appraisal information can also be studied in order to determine training needs. My observation, asking and listening, the manager can conduct a performance analysis. The specific steps and performance analysis include the following. Aye, aye, praised the performance of employees in order to determine how they're doing in comparison with how they should be doing and determine behavioral discrepancies. They assess the cost and value of correcting a behavioral discrepancy. See, determine if it is a can't do or won't do situation, it is important to determine if the employee could do the expected job if he or she wanted to.

The set standards because underperformance might result if an employee does not know what the standards are. E remove obstacles relating to time, equipment and people which result in behavior discrepancies. Allow the employees time to practice so that he or she can perform the job better. Do provide training if the performance analysis indicates that knowledge, skills or attitudes need to be altered. Age redesigned the job through job enrichment, job simplification or enlargement, if necessary, to improve performance. I transfer or terminate employee services if all else has failed. J great, a motivational climate, sometimes a skilled employee does not want to perform the job because of motivational problems. Rewards, punishment, discipline or some combination may be needed to create a positive climate for the optimal use of skills. Presenting training programs.

After training needs have been determined, specific and measurable objectives must be established for meeting these needs. Effective training objectives should state what the organization, department or individual should achieve once training is completed. For example, to improve listening and feedback skills for use in the performance appraisal program. Training objectives can be categorized as instructional objectives, what facts, principles and concepts are to be learned in the training program? Who is to be taught, when are they to be taught? Organizational and departmental objectives.

What impact will the training have on organizational and mental outcomes such as absenteeism, turnover costs and productivity? Individual performance and growth objectives. What impact will the training program have on the attitudes, behavior and personal growth of the trainee? What should he or she be able to do after the training? Under what conditions should the training be able to perform the trained behavior? How well should the training perform the trained behavior? Explicit objectives serve a number of purposes. They assist in developing the criteria to be used in evaluating the training outcome.

Together, training objectives and evaluation criteria also help in choosing relevant instructional material. During training objectives help motivate trainees to organize their efforts in a way that will help them accomplish those objectives. Before a training program is presented, the presenter should ensure that sound learning principles are followed to maximize learning. Then the training methods that are most applicable for the specific situation must be selected. Maximization for learning.

We're training to have any effect at all, trainees must learn something from it. When training is effectively designed and trainees are motivated, learning can occur.

The use of sound learning principles during the development and implementation of training programs contributes to its success. Ability to learn. Individuals enter training with different experiences, different levels of familiarity with the material and different mental and physical abilities. The training demands should match the abilities of trainees. Training that is too difficult or too easy is likely to be less effective. Testing trainees prior to beginning training can help ensure a good match. Motivation to learn. In order to learn, a person must want to learn. Perhaps the most important motivation trainees bring to training is their desire to change their behavior and the results on the job. In the context of training, motivation, influence is a person's enthusiasm for training, keeps attention focused on training activities and reinforces what is learned.

People strive to achieve objectives they have set for themselves. The objectives of employees include job security financially and intellectually rewarding work recognition, status, responsibility and achievement. The learning process is facilitated when the training program helps employees to achieve these objectives. Supportive supervisors and the expectation that training results will be assessed later on the job contribute to higher training motivation. Goal setting. Individuals' conscious goals may regulate their behavior. The trainer's job is to get the trainees to adopt two or internalize the goals of the program in the following ways. A can make learning objectives at the outset, and that very strategic points throughout the training program. They make goals difficult enough to be a challenge. See, supplement the overall goals with some goals to maintain feelings of accomplishment.

Reinforcement

The idea behind the reinforcement is that behavior appearing to lead to a positive consequence tends to be repeated, while behavior leading to a negative consequence tends not to be repeated. Learners must be rewarded for new behavior in ways that satisfy needs such as pay, praise, recognition and promotion. For example, a trainee who was praised for good performance is likely to continue to strive for additional praise. According to the expectancy theory, individuals are motivated to choose behavior that is the greatest chance of producing desired consequences. Trainers must believe that acquiring the knowledge and skills from training will lead to desired outcomes and that training can provide that knowledge or skill.

Low of the training program. Each segment of the training should be organized so that the individual can see not only its purpose, but also how it fits in with the other parts of the program. Later, segments should build on those presented earlier. Modeling and self efficacy. The trainer can build training skills by allowing them to see models of good and poor performance and by giving trainees confidence in their abilities to apply their skills. Confidence building includes providing trainees with encouragement, guidance and feedback on how well they're doing and providing the opportunity for practice.

Practice and repetition. Learning requires time to assimilate what has been learned, to accept it, internalize it, and to build confidence in what has been learned. This requires practice and repetition of the material. After sufficient practice, the skills may become automatic, requiring little conscious thought. Trainees should be given opportunities to continue practicing even after they've achieved proficiency for the first time. All we're learning leads to a relative permanent change in behavior and automatic responses to the learning task. Spacing of sessions. Training spread out over a period of time facilitates the learning process. The interval most conducive to learning depends on the type of training. Material must be meaningful.

Appropriate material for sequential learning, for example, cases, problems, discussion outlines and reading lists must be provided. The learning methods used should be as varied as possible. Boredom destroys learning. Any method that is overused will begin to bore learners. Small training units. The learning material should be presented in small segments or units. This format allows quick feedback to the training on how well he or she is doing. All or part of training. Learning is facilitated when an overview is given to trainees and then divided into portions for in-depth instruction. Whether to use whole or part learning depends also on the difficulty of the task and the degree of relationship between subtasks. Transfer of learning.

The trainer must do his or her best to make the training as close to the reality of the job as possible to ensure that the newly learned behavior is transferred to the work environment. Knowledge of results. Knowledge of results, feedback influences the learning process. Keeping employees informed of their progress as measured against some standard helps in setting goals for what remains to be learned. The process of analyzing progress and establishing new objectives enhances learning. Precautions should be taken that goals are not so difficult to achieve, that employees become discouraged. The characteristics of the instructional environment and instructors.

The instructional environment can be designed around events such as gaining attention, informing learners of objectives, presenting the training stimulus material, providing feedback, assessing performance and enhancing retention and transfer. The instructor should have informed everyone around the facilities, checked the physical requirements, secured the necessary equipment, established training objectives, and studied the Chapter plan to anticipate group responses and to prepare experiences. Training methods that can be used can be classified as onset methods and offsite methods. Onsite training methods include the following. On the job training.

On the job, training is probably the most widely used method of training. The employee is placed into the real work situation and she's on the job and the tricks of the trade by an experienced employee or the supervisor. Although this program is simple and relatively inexpensive, if it is not handled properly, the cost can be high and damaged machinery, unsatisfied customers and poorly trained employees. To prevent these problems, Trainor's must be carefully selected and trained. The trainees should be placed with a trainer with similar background and personality. The trainer should be motivated by training and be rewarded for doing it while.

Apprentice training. Apprentice training is a combination of on site and off site training. It requires the cooperation of the employer. Trainers at the workplace and technical training institutions. The Apprentice commits to a period of training and learning that involves both formal classroom learning and practical on the job experience. Vestibule training. Industrial training, the trainee learns the job in an environment that simulates the real working environment as closely as possible. For example, training of pilots in a simulated cockpit of an airplane. A machine operator training might run a machine under the supervision of a trainer until he or she learns how to use it properly.

Only then is the trainee sent to the shop for. This procedure can be quite expensive if the number of trainees supervised is not large. Coaching and counseling. One of the best and most frequently used methods of training new managers is for effective managers to teach them. The coach sets a good example of what a manager does, answers questions and explains why things are done the way they are. It is the court's obligation to see to it that the manager trainee makes the proper contacts so that the job can be easily and performed in an adequate way. Although most organizations use coaching and counseling as an informal management development technique, it has problems.

Coaching and counseling failed when inadequate time was set aside for them when the subordinate is not allowed to make mistakes, if rivalry develops or if the dependency needs of the trainee are not recognized and accepted by the manager. Computer based training. Computer based training permits self-paced learning and immediate feedback. This type of training works as follows: a training set at a terminal with a monitor. The computer is programmed with the training materials. To communicate by programming or using the keyboard to input commands or requests.

The advantages of computer based training include availability, self-paced features, distribution and adaptability and work simulation. Job rotation. Trainees can be rotated through a series of jobs to broaden their managerial experience. Organizations often have developed career plans that include a mix of functional and geographic transfers. Because of the perceived relevance of on the job experience, onsite training methods should be used in training programs. Job development programs should, however, supplement them where expertise is not readily available.

Offside training methods include Chapters. In a Chapter, an instructor presents material to a group of learners, Chapters are relatively inexpensive to develop and deliver. You can import factual knowledge quickly and efficiently. Chapters, however, lead to one way communication, are insensitive towards learning differences and do not allow feedback to the trainer. Many of these difficulties can be overcome by a competent Chapter who makes use of discussions during the Chapter. Conference. The conference is a participative method that emphasizes small group discussion in which the instructor guides rather than instructs trainees. Through a process of questions and answers and discussions to a desired outcome.

The objectives of the conference method are to develop problem solving and decision making skills, present new and complex material and modify attitudes. Topics for discussion can be chosen by the instructor or by trainee's. The leader of the session prepares for the topic in advance of the session. The training may be given an agenda for the meeting or may develop it on their own. The conference method requires a high degree of participation from the trainees and provides immediate feedback and the opportunity to assess own learning by listening to the comments made by the instructor and other group participants.

The conference method is limited in the amount of substance of material that can be covered in one chapter. It also requires trainees with good verbal skills and self images so that they are not threatened by group participation. Audio, video and teleconferencing. Recordings, films and chapters can be distributed to learners and used independently or in conjunction with other training. It is possible to produce effective videos at low cost. The advantage of audio visual techniques is their ability to quickly distribute a consistent training experience to a large number of individuals without being constrained by the time limits of instructors on the gist, the requirements. With video teleconferencing, learners are in remote classrooms equipped with televisions and microphones.

The instructor provides the training from a video studio often linked to learners via satellite. Learners can see the instructor and ask questions via audio links to the studio. Audio teleconferencing provides a similar arrangement that uses only audio connections. Programming instruction. For them, instruction presents the learner with a series of tasks, allows evaluation of success and intervals throughout training, and provides feedback about correct and incorrect responses as the learner advances through the training. One instruction can be incorporated into books, machines and computers. Careful attention must be given to learning sequences and objectives. Learners progress faster with programmed instruction than with Chapters. Other advantages of programmed instruction are that materials can be packaged and distributed.

Self-Paced Learning

Learners can use the material at their convenience and when they are ready. It also makes provision for self-paced learning, which allows flexibility according to different abilities. Learning by doing. Learning by doing training techniques copy the essential elements of real world situations. They allow learners to play a role or make decisions about the situation and then receive feedback about their effectiveness. Business games allow learners to make decisions about business variables, often competing against other individuals or teams. The case study presents learners with a written report of a realistic situation. The learners analyze the information and prepare solutions for discussion. Role playing involves having trainers act out simulated roles.

Interpersonal skills can be learned by using roles. Advantages of these training methods include the potential for a high degree of transfer to the work situation. I participate in involvement, providing specific feedback and helping learners deal with incomplete information. Evaluating training and development programs. It is necessary to evaluate training programs. Most effective programs can be withdrawn to save time and effort. Weaknesses within established programs can be identified and remedy. One way to approach the evaluation of training programs is according to the model of Kirkpatrick. According to Kirkpatrick, training programs can be evaluated on four levels, namely reaction, learning, behavior and results. Focus, nine point two.

Kirkpatrick, levels of evaluation of training programs. Reaction. Evaluating the reaction of a training program answers the following question. How well did the trainees like the program? Reaction evaluation should consider topics such as program content, program structure and format, instructional techniques, instructor abilities and style. Quality of the learning environment, extending to training objectives were achieved and recommendations for improvement. Reaction evaluations done directly after the training program or a few weeks thereafter. The shortcoming of reaction evaluation is that the enthusiasm of trainees cannot necessarily be taken as evidence of improved ability and performance. Learning.

Evaluating the learning after a training program answers the following question: what facts, principles and concepts were learned in the training program? Learning evaluation is concerned with how well the facts, principles and skills were understood by trainees. Paper and pencil or skill tests can be used to evaluate learning. In order to obtain an accurate picture of what was learned, trainees should be tested before and after the training program. Behavior. Evaluating the behavior of trainees after a training program answers the following question. The job behavior of trainees changes because of the program. A systematic appraisal should be made on the job performance on a before and after basis.

The appraisal of performance should be made by the trainer, the trainee superior, their subordinates or their peers. A statistical analysis should be made to compare performance before and after the training program and to relate changes to the training program. The post training appraisal should be made several months after the training so that the trainees have an opportunity to put into practice what they have learned. An experimental group will receive training and a control group who do not receive training should be used. Evaluating the results of a training program answers the following question. What were the results of the program in terms of costs and productivity? Activity, nine point one.

The recent training and development perspective and one hundred year old Krater. The development and empowerment process has overtaken the training event in organizations. The focus is on learning through reframing the workplace problems, self-determined developments and freezing barriers to learning and understanding what it means to be a learning organization. However, if we investigate the life and philosophy of Dr Y Siegel, it is evident that this approach is not so new. Dr. YFC James was born in China in 1890 three. He dedicated his life to mass education and rural reconstruction, first in China and then throughout the world.

He committed himself to sensitizing the world's intellectual community, the tremendous losses the world suffered by ignoring the humanity of the poor and by not acknowledging their productivity. During the First World War, he was stationed in France to supervise Chinese laborers. While there, he realized that the people's illiteracy was no fault of their own. He proclaimed, I began to realize that what these humble, common people of my country lacked was not brains, for God has given that to them, but opportunity. They are potential powers waiting for a development, waiting for them. If one considers the principles of adult learning, the training cycle and training methods, the above observation of James is still applicable today.

James and develop the cradle of rural reconstruction, portraying the developmental approach that should be applied, the credo speaks as follows. Go to the people, live among them, learn from them, run with them, work with them. Start with what they know, build on what they have. Teach by showing, learn by doing. Not a showcase, but a pattern, not odds and ends, but a system not to conform, but to transform, not really believe. James. Critical thinking activity. Can you apply the approach portrayed in the credo to training and development approaches in the workplace? How? Summary.

Induction has been defined as the introduction of new employees to the organization, work unit and job. The idea was expressed that it should be grouped with human resource management activities and subjects of study, such as training and development, because orientation involves learning. The objectives of induction seem to be learning job procedures, establishing relationships with co-workers and fitting into the new employer's way of doing things. To give the employee a sense of belonging and to create favorable attitudes towards the company. Both the personnel and human resource departments and line managers and supervisors are responsible for induction.

The contents of an induction program can be divided into general organizational aspects and specific Department of job aspects. Induction programs should regularly be followed up and evaluated. Training is a form of job specific education directed at improving the knowledge, skills and attitudes of employees. Effective organizations designed their training programs after assessing the individuals and organizations training needs and setting training objectives. Effective training programs select trainees on the basis of their needs, as well as the objectives of the organization.

Various training methods can be used, sound learning principles should, however, be employed to maximize trainees learning. It is, however, important that training Books be evaluated to determine the reaction of participants, to evaluate the learning achieved, behavioral changes effected, and the impact on work results after the completion of the training Book. Key concepts and terms. Apprentice training behavior. Coaching. Computer based training. Connotes. Counseling. Declarative knowledge development. Education. Induction. Job rotation. Knowledge. Learning by doing. Learning Principles Chapter.

On the job training, performance analysis, procedural knowledge, programmed instruction, reaction. Results. Teleconferencing training. Training cycle, training needs training objectives. That's to be training. Sample surtitles. What are the main objectives of an induction program for new employees? Why are training programs one of the first areas to be eliminated when an organization's budget is cut? If you were asked to develop a training program for taxi drivers, how would you do it? How would you evaluate the training program?

How to Deal with Tough Times

Life is not always simple and straight, as every one of us expects. Most of the time, you have to face many challenges, which makes your life miserable. This Book is about how to deal with tough times in your life. I am in my. And we'll share the information related to solving your problems and to deal with the tough times before moving further.

Let me tell you a short story of two farmers who cultivate the potatoes. The first farmer asked a question to the second one, then how do you sort the potatoes before going into the market? As there were, there were different prices for small, medium and large potatoes.

The other farmer replied that I just put the potatoes in the truck and tools that assist Drew who are in the market. After 10 kilometers, Small potatoes go down and make potatoes come up just due to the difficulties and hardship of the broken loans. The answer of the second former. He's also relevant to our daily lives, and he does that home we should be with during tough times. We should remember that when it is tough to get to, it means tough.

Rightly Analysis of Problem

Analyze the problem and write to me. Makes it easy for you to identify the right solution. Let's discuss some basics that will help you correctly analyze a problem, first of all, that everyone has the problems. And you are not the only one in this world who is facing a problem. The second thing that will help you to realize the problem, that every problem has a limited time span. Therefore, you should not be disappointed in the situation you are facing and give your full attention towards the analysis of your problem. There can be some positive aspects related to a problem as well. For example, heavy rain in town may create problems for a person due to the flooding. However, it may create the opportunity for the Tantalus. Another example that you may have heard of in honor of Microsoft, Bill Gates was not hired by a company just due to non-availability of the e-mail address. And this issue or this problem led him to start his own business.

Underestimating the Problem

In this chapter, you will learn how you can manage the problem. The first step to manage a problem is always. Your problem, seriously, I never underestimated. For example, If you're eating junk food on a daily basis, it will definitely increase your weight. Or. If you're drunk driving in the area and thinking that it will not hurt you, it will be a big mistake.

Waiting for Miracle

Miracles happen in this world, but not with everyone. Therefore, Never beat. For example, if you have doubleness, don't sit in front of your elephant. And there someone will call you who offers a job. Then I mean, your problem is you analyze it and identify the best solution and start moving to the.

Anger on Root Cause of Problem

The turbulence declared to manage the problem is not to get angry at the root cause of the problem. For example, if you are missing nuclear bombs. Never say that you are an idiot who is willing to terminate my job. Remember that, and that always makes things complex. It will lead you to make big wrong decisions. Therefore, always try to fix the problem, not the responsibility.

Look around to know Who else has same problem

Key element to many, the problem is that you should look around to see who else had the same problem that you're facing right now. Oh, no. You can see a friend of yours. His name is Edward. Well, also fired from his job due to short term plumbing. Afterward, he fixed the temperament issue and applied to another company where he is working fine. The people who have already experienced the same problems that you are facing right now can help you to manage the problem and wait for the right solution.

Prepare your Bait

Now moving towards the final words related to managing the problem. All of us are going to defy your problem and prepare the right be vulnerable if you have a degree in petroleum engineering and good governance because there is no oil related McKenzies in your city, then you shouldn't look around on the map and identify the location or areas where the relevant McKenzies could be available before your CV and start counting the job where we can simulate.

Keep Communicating

Communication with others is a key factor to reduce the impact of problems and to many, many of them effectively. We should always remember that guards believe in solving a problem doesn't mean the God denied there to be optimistic and. Try to focus on the principles we discussed many of the problems.

Exaggerating the Problem

And the key principle to manage the problems effectively. Is there never exaggerating the problem? As you can see in this picture. The girl is looking at her shadow. And thinking that she is too bulky. And it is impossible to reduce it. Remember, that exaggeration of a problem will make you disappointed. And instead of going for resolution, you were trying to start avoiding the problem.

What is Leadership

In the U.S., we discussed how to manage the problem. Now we are going to discuss how we can solve the problem. To solve the problem, there are two major steps. No one. Taking the leadership. To deal with obstacles. And the second step to solve the problem is to adopt the thinking. A question may arise in your mind at what is leadership? And why it is required to solve the problem. During problem solving, you may find you may get into situations where you need to make difficult decisions, therefore you should have the leadership abilities to handle the situation. In the next few chapters, we are going to discuss the leadership principles that will help you to solve the problem.

Surrendering Leadership to Faces

The first principle is never surrender your leadership to the fishes. For example, If you and your next door neighbor both are working. Two organizations. Which are competitors to each of them? And any idea presented by you can harm the company of your neighbor. But you remain away from presenting your idea just because your neighbor may feel it is better.

Surrendering Leadership to Fences

The second principle of leadership is never surrender your leadership to the fences. Which means that never, ever limit your thoughts to a single point. You solve the problem. For example, If your dream job is available in China and there is no direct flight available to China, which will make it impossible for you to get a dream job in this situation, you may identify some alternate routes. Which may have difficulties. Along with extra expenses. However they may have done that to you. I'll take you into China. And to get a job there.

Surrendering Leadership to Frustration

Third principle of leadership is to never surrender the leadership to the frustrations, keep in mind that whoever has high dreams has to face the frustrations. For example, if you are preparing for a final exam, but there is a lot of noise outside. In this situation, you need to find some place in your house which is away from the street, or you can start studying when all the people around you are sleeping. Likewise, if you are working in an office and you have to prepare a presentation for your boss, but you are not getting time to finish it. In this situation, you may get. Frustrated. Which will ultimately add any delay to complete your work. For any situation where you are getting frustrated, you have to show leadership skills and manage the frustration.

Surrendering Leadership to Fears

Another principle of leadership is that never surrender the leadership to the fierce. For example, if you want to buy a house in a specific area, but. You are not doing so as you think their people may laugh at you due to the high price you pay for that area. Or if you want to start a business, but are afraid of failure. All of you are not quitting your job just because of the fear you get filled in the new place. Or someone may not be applying for the admission test of medical college just due to the fear of failure. Or you're not shifting to the new city, even though there are a lot of opportunities just because of fear that you will lose your friends. Remember, surrendering your leadership to fear will ultimately create new problems for you.

Surrendering Leadership to Fatigue

Another principle of leadership is to never surrender your leadership to the freed. Sometimes solving the problem demands additional efforts to be put in. In any situation where you are looking tired. Take a small break. But do not do not lose your stamina. And momentum.

Possibility Thinking

Second step towards resolution of the problem is to adopt the possibility of thinking. Or in simple words, thinking out of the box. Possibility thinking is related to enlisting all types of possible solutions to your problem. Let's discuss a few principles. That will help you to adopt the possibility, thinking no one will ever reject a possibility or a possible solution if it seems wrong to you or you are not sure about if it will work or not. Number two, never reject a possible solution to your problem, if anyone else. Mitic, it's credit. Number three, never reject an idea just because someone or they're already doing the same, there is no harm in copying the idea to solve your problem. Number four, never reject a solution or idea if you believe it is not possible in the current scenario. Never reject a possibility if you are, you already have planned your line of action, always be open.

To adopt alternatives, even though you have defined or you have planned what line of action you want to take. Never reject an idea. If it is currently illegal, for example, if you are trying to sell a product that is illegal in a state, there are chances that another state does not have. Same legal issues. For that product and you can move to that state where it is not illegal to sell it, never reject a possible solution just because you don't have money. The next principle towards possibility, thinking they're never rejecting any idea just because it may create conflicts with your friends or with your family. For example, if you are going to start a new business. But do think that whenever you will put the idea in front of your family. They will start conflicting with you. For any such situation, you have to manage the conflict politely and wisely, but you should not give up to proceed with the solution of your problem.

Summary

Now, let's discuss the summary of how to deal with tough times: No one and lies the problem as well as its root cause. Write down every single possible solution to your problem. For each possible solution right down the line of action time it may take and challenges associated with that solution. Select the best suitable solution for the further execution work to remove the hindrances related to choosing a solution. Start taking action. And in case you get seen, just realize the problem and identify any other solution to go on. All of us remember people who keep trying. Definitely take it to the destination.

Additional Chapter-Compound Effect

In this chapter, we're going to discuss the compound effect. Compound effect is actually referred to the small but country's Hebert's that make a big impact on your life. If you see the picture. That is available on your screen. You can see that this is a picture of a blusher. However, every one of you will be well aware. That glaciers never come into existence within this. All Galicia's came into existence due to constant and continuous. Snowfall. Here are a few examples of compound effects, for example. If you take a piece of pink pig on a daily basis. It will add multiple layers of fabric in your body. And if you get bulky. You will become a slow learner and your performance in the office will also decrease. And if you are a slow learner. An unknown performer in your office.

It may be. The words termination of your job. In this example, you can see there is one bad habit of eating. Extra sugar on a daily basis. Can create multiple problems in your life, including obesity, slow learning and the dog termination. Let's discuss and then probe another example of compound effect, that, for example, if you read. Few pages of a book every day. It will take a lot of knowledge and will develop. A reliable knowledge base in your mind. Which will ultimately improve your personality. And because of that, you've been promoted. A small and continuous habit on a regular basis. Make clear its larger impact on your life. In positive or negative, this always tries to adopt positive habits.

Which will make your life easier and will and will keep you away from the tough times. Now, let's look at how that works. There are 300 years of companies that, number one, have small choices. Less consistency. And the third one is the. All these ingredients. The compound effect, Anjali's. Be patient. And continue your practice, which will ultimately give you the right solution. So keep working with full passion. And the little question then, is everything possible with the help of complicit? Answer is, yes, you can achieve everything with the help of burning desire. For example, if you see a severe bombing in an area, you will never enter the area. However, if you see there, your child is stuck in that area. Zober, definitely. Run towards the. Area where you saw the bombings, strong burning desire keeps you motivated to work with consistency and achieve the benefit of compound effect.

Agile Leadership: Become An Agile Leader

Hello and welcome. It's great to have you on the Book here. Together we'll be exploring Agile. This is both a way of managing projects and an approach to work that breaks from the more traditional organizational structures many of us are familiar with, like top down leadership and siloed teams. Though Agile started in software development, it doesn't have to be used only on IT projects. In fact, organizations across all sorts of sectors want to improve their organizational agility to help their teams work better, faster and much happier too. This Book has been designed for people who are new to Agile, who want to take a leadership role with their team and start to use agile principles and processes in their work. You don't need to have an official management role to start implementing Agile.

We've built the Book for people who have an aptitude for leadership but don't necessarily have a formal leadership role. You can lead a team from within and you don't need official power to help a team work in an agile way. What you need is influence. You also don't have to be a project manager to use Agile, although it is a valuable framework for managing projects. Your team might be made up of people who have very different specialisms, but that doesn't matter. Agile is an approach to collaborative and open work where people can share their ideas and skills, make time to learn and feel invested in their work.

These approaches create opportunities for people with different backgrounds and skill sets to work together and develop better products. You may be working from inside a traditional organization and wondering, Can I implement Agile here? The answer is a resounding yes. One of the best ways to create a more agile organization is by starting small in one team or department and championing the cause. Ultimately, to get the best out of an Agile approach, you'll want the whole organization to work this way. Still, we've all gotta start somewhere, so create an opportunity for you and your team to become the shining example of agility within the company.

During this Book, we'll be explaining some of the fundamental principles and practices that Agile teams use. We'll be helping you put together an Agile leadership plan that will support your professional development and help you put your own Agile team together. Here's what we'll cover. chapter one Introducing Agile here. We'll find out what Agile is and what capabilities, traits, skills and habits an Agile leader should be looking for. chapter two Why Agile? In this chapter we'll find out the benefits of Agile and what an Agile leader looks like. chapter three Build your awareness. In this chapter, you'll reflect on your skills and capabilities and those of your team. chapter four Develop your ideas.

Here you'll discover opportunities to implement Agile ways of working and try them out in your own context. chapter five Make a commitment. Finally, you'll complete your Agile leadership plan, putting some commitments in place for actions you will take towards your leadership goals. Are you ready? Let's get started. I hope you enjoy this Book and I will see you again soon. Good luck.

What Is Agile?

What does Agile mean in the first place? Well, Agile is a different way of working. You don't have to follow a framework or set rules. Sure, there are processes and practices that Agile practitioners like to use, but at its core, agility means thinking differently about your organization's culture. You take on tasks and interact with your team in a new way. Agile is based on transparency, collaboration and autonomy. Teams deliver value frequently by organizing themselves rather than taking direction from senior managers. Agile started in software development with the 2001 Agile Manifesto created by a small group of developers who wanted to find a shared way of working. The values they chose are number one. Individuals and interactions over processes and tools. Number two. Working software over comprehensive documentation.

Number three. Customer collaboration over contract negotiation. Number four, responding to change over following a plan. What do these mean? Let's take a closer look. Our first value individuals and interactions over processes and tools tells us that it doesn't matter what the tools or processes are that we use to do our work. What matters is the people. Bringing the right people together and giving them the space to interact with each other to solve the problems is one of the driving ideas behind Agile. Our second value states working software over comprehensive documentation. Now we can swap software for products. Agile is used across sectors. It isn't just the domain of the IT department anymore.

But if you look at traditional ways of managing projects like Waterfall, you'll find a lot of time is spent up front discussing and planning and documenting a project. Having a plan is no bad thing, but what matters is getting a working product into your customer's hands so that you can find out if it works for them and get feedback to improve the next release. This is why Agile teams focus on rapid development with testing and learning built into the process rather than a lot of upfront planning, which slows the team down and makes it harder to respond to changes.

Our next value is customer collaboration over contract negotiation. You could spend a lot of time tweaking the fine details of a contract, only to find that by the time the product is built, the customer's changing requirements, testing, feedback and market forces have resulted in a different product than you originally planned. So instead of spending so much time on trying to set the project scope in stone, agile teams focus on continuous development, creating a feedback loop so that the customer's feedback is firmly part of the design process. Our final value is responding to change by following a plan which relates to what we've just talked about.

The circumstances we're working with are constantly changing. So instead of creating a rigid process plan, we need to accept and expect these shifting priorities. So give your team space to pivot in a new direction when it makes sense to do so. Each team has their own way of implementing Agile methodologies, so your choices will be unique to you. But the 12 principles of Agile should always guide your decisions. Here they are. Principle number one Our highest priority is to satisfy the customer through early and continuous delivery. Principle number two welcomes changing requirements even in late development. Agile processes harness change for the customer's competitive advantage.

Principle number three Deliver projects frequently from a couple of weeks to a couple of months with a preference for a shorter timescale. Principle number four Coordinating team members must work together daily through the project. Principle number five Build projects around motivated individuals. Give them the environment and support they need and trust them to get the job done. Principle number six A face to face conversation is the most efficient and effective method of conveying information to and within different teams. Principle number seven The final product is the primary measure of progress. Principle number eight Agile processes promote sustainable development.

All stakeholders should be able to maintain a constant pace indefinitely. Principle number nine Continuous attention to technical excellence and good design enhances agility. Principle number ten. Simplicity. The art of maximizing the amount of work not done is essential. Principle number 11 The best architectures, requirements and designs emerge from self-organizing teams. And finally, principle number 12. At regular intervals, the team reflects on becoming more effective then tunes and adjusts its behavior accordingly. Part of becoming an Agile leader is developing an agile mindset. Over time, you will naturally gravitate towards doing things in an agile way.

You can't shift the way you think overnight, but let's get you thinking this way from the start so that it's an easier transition for you as you meet and share ideas with other agile practitioners, you'll find that Agile can be a bit of an obsession, innovating and steadily delivering customer value. Getting work done in a focused way with small self-organized teams and collaborating across a network. These are all things that preoccupy agile leaders and you might count yourself among them soon. Next, let's find out how well you and your team are using these principles right now.

Reflect On The Principles Of Agile

Throughout this Book, you'll be doing some exercises aimed at helping you to understand where you and your team and your organization are in terms of agility, to make practical changes in the way you work and improve your performance as an agile leader. You'll need a plan. So let's start putting one together. We'll focus on your own professional development, but we'll also look at what you can do more widely within your team to implement agile successfully. We've created an Agile Leadership Plan template for you that you can download. It gives you space to complete the exercises we'll mention throughout the Book. Your first exercise is a short check in to see how agile your team is now. Don't worry if the conclusion is not very.

That's why you're here. But it will be easier to plan for where you are headed once you have a clear idea of where you are at. Your first exercise to complete in your plan is to take a few moments to think about and make some notes on the 12 principles of Agile. Which of the principles do you think are being used actively by your team now? How could you implement the principles that are not being used at the moment? What resources, people and support would you need to do so? Try to identify at least one action for yourself and one for your team based on your responses. When you're ready, move on to the next chapter to find out how the agile mindset will set you apart from teams that operate in a more traditional way.

Agile Mindset

What does it mean to have an Agile mindset? Well, in traditional organizations, there's usually a group of senior managers in charge who have a group of middle managers working under them. They in turn have junior managers and teams working under them. Strategic direction comes from the senior management information and requests flow downwards from the senior managers to the employees, but rarely upwards. Employees do as they are required to do, and once they finish a project, the cycle begins again. Is this how things work in your organization? In these environments, projects start with a lot of planning and documentation, but if requirements change or something changes in the market, while teams are working through a project that has been meticulously planned up front, it's not so easy to adapt in these more traditional organizations. Managers are most interested in making money for the company and its shareholders.

They determine the rules and the roles and pass these down for the employees to implement. That's not to say hierarchical organizations don't care about the customer. Many of them do. But there is a lot of bureaucracy involved in this sort of structure, which does tend to slow things down so that it's harder to meet market demands in a hurry. In a traditional organization, maximizing value for the shareholder is the core goal. While in Agile organizations, delivering value to the customer is the focus. In traditional organizations, people report to bosses who define the roles, rules and performance.

But in an Agile organization, small self-organizing teams set their own agendas.

These two types of organizations are quite different in structure to a top down hierarchy with siloed departments is what we'd expect in a traditional structure. But in an Agile organization, there is a network of teams in a flatter structure who collaborate and work towards a shared vision. People can easily move around the organization to where they are needed most, and interdepartmental teams can come together when employees across an organization think in a traditional way, this creates a very different and more rigid way of working than an agile mindset shared by many across an organization.

So if your aspirations amount to having an Agile team, if you'd like to see an entirely agile organization emerge, you will need to engage leaders across the other teams too. But the best place to start is with yourself and your team. This will help you to set an example which will help you to nudge the other teams towards agility before you move on to the next chapter. Please complete the exercise. How agile is your team to get a sense of where you are starting from? You will find this in your Agile Leadership plan supporting document.

What Does It Mean To Be An Agile Business?

You now have a sense of what your team's starting point is, but it's also helpful to look at the business as a whole. At an organizational level, agile businesses can adapt quickly to changes in the market and respond flexibly to what customers want because they are able to bring the right people together and give them the space to do their best work. This creates an ongoing competitive advantage. An Agile organization is viewed not as a static machine in the way that organizations traditionally might be, but as an organism that is alive and constantly changing. Here's what that looks like. See how the traditional organizational machine has a clear hierarchy with bureaucracy occupying the space between upper management and the teams.

You'll also notice that teams are in silos, each with a homogenous group of people. Now, if we look at the organization as an organism, some teams are mixed, each containing different people with different capabilities or specialisms, with some people working across multiple teams or on their own edges. Leaders are in the middle acting as enablers in this organism structure. You can see just from looking at the visual representation, that this is a much more collaborative and flexible way of working. Here are five key elements of an Agile organization. According to McKinsey and Company number one strategy. Number two structure.

Number three Process. Number four people. Number five, technology. Let's take a look at each of these in more detail.

Everyone across an Agile organization shares the same purpose and vision. Resources are allocated in a flexible way so that teams can respond to opportunities when they come up. Agile organizations are constantly looking for feedback from their stakeholders and they put the customer at the center of what they do, always looking for ways to better serve themselves. Using customer insights, they design, pilot, launch and iterate new products. An agile organization tends to be flat rather than hierarchical. Senior managers provide actionable guidance. Roles are clear and teams partner up to share knowledge, skills and even people openly. Agile organizations build their processes around performance.

Contrary to what you might think, there are processes in agile environments, but these are designed to enable creativity and innovation, not hinder them by loosely defining processes at a high level. Agile organizations can share information and assure quality while leaving space for teams to design their own ways of working. The organization can communicate and adopt best practices widely and if employees switch teams or roles even temporarily, they can do so without much disruption. Agile organizations make decisions actively so that they can rapidly experiment and learn. They work in short, focused sprints and are interested in developing minimum viable products to test and learn from, rather than designing lengthy processes around building polished but untested products that may not be successful in the marketplace.

People in agile organizations are entrepreneurially minded. They are given autonomy and the freedom to pursue learning opportunities. Leaders serve their teams rather than managing them in the traditional sense. The focus is on developing people and creating a cohesive and dynamic community. Technology is an enabler in an agile organization. Next generation tools evolve as necessary. Rather than using inflexible tools that are not fit for purpose in the long term, Agile businesses particularly benefit from digital tools that enable real time communication and work management, enabling collaboration across time zones and locations seamlessly. Now that you know what Agile is and how it represents a mindset shift from the more traditional ways of working, you are ready to explore your own context and find out what Agile can do for you. When you're ready, let's move on to chapter two.

What Makes Agile Successful?

In the previous chapter, we looked at what Agile is and what it takes to have an Agile mindset. Maybe you're thinking, Well, that sounds a lot like my team already. If so, you are well on your way to becoming an Agile organization and getting the benefits of this way of working. But if Agile feels like quite a departure for you, you might wonder why put time and energy into changing the way we work? Well, agile teams and organizations get a lot of benefits, as we've already discovered. They can respond quickly to market changes, releasing products before more traditional competitors do, and making changes to their offerings based on what the customers are asking for.

Naturally, the company that moves faster to solve a problem, create a product or respond to a need, will be the business that wins by focusing on minimum viable products that they can test and learn from. They avoid spending a lot of time and money building a product that might not work. Instead, they get feedback from customers all the way along, iterating as they go so that there is a high probability of success when their product hits the market. This leads to a far better customer experience because the customer and other stakeholders are involved in the development process.

Agility makes it possible to work more quickly because teams work in short focused sprints where the goal is to produce a product or increment of value. This tends to eliminate a lot of busy work using technology and standardized processes to enable communication across the organization while giving teams the autonomy to make their own decisions. Also helps agile organizations to avoid a lot of the bureaucracy that can cost traditional organizations time. Another area where Agile really shines relates to people. If an organization wants to attract top talent, it has to have a value proposition that is hard to beat. A truly agile working environment attracts passionate and engaged candidates by reputation and offering flexibility, autonomy and opportunities for growth.

By nature, agile organizations have great networks, both internally and externally, and in this way they become aware of and can reach out to in-demand talent before competing organizations snap them up. The well being of employees is paramount in an Agile organization. They tend to be much more flexible because people are trusted and accountable to each other. So set working hours or locations are not always the norm. This flexibility increases employee motivation and job satisfaction. These businesses invest in their people, helping them to build new skills as a natural part of what they do. One of the best ways to contribute to people's mental health is to ensure their work is meaningful and purposeful.

Organizations as a whole can provide meaning due to the mission they serve. Nonprofits and social organizations have an advantage here, but this feeling of doing meaningful work can exist even in commercial ventures. As long as people feel like they are making a valuable contribution to their customers' lives. Agile focuses on creating value that builds this naturally. Agile is built on delivering value in small increments, and this is a great opportunity to celebrate small wins. This can be as simple as giving a verbal thank you or adding a post to a shared notice board. But you'll notice that when employees feel like other people are grateful for what they're doing and their hard work gets noticed, that has a positive impact on well-being. Before you move on to the next chapter, reflect on what opportunities you think that Agile could create for your organization.

What could it do for the commercial viability of your organization? How might it impact your ability to innovate? How might it change your customer engagement processes? What about marketing and sales? What will it do for your people and the air? Could it impact your ability to recruit and retain talented people? How could it improve the well-being of your employees? As you identify these opportunities, this will help you to get buy-in from your team and others in the organization if you need to. They'll form a key part of why you're becoming agile as a leader and a team. There's space for you to make some notes in your Agile leadership plan. When you've completed your reflection, move on to the next chapter to explore the traits of successful agile leaders.

What Makes An Agile Leader?

Now that you know what an Agile organization could look like and you have a vision for the potential of your own organization, we've got to start with you. How can you become a more agile leader? The Agile leadership approach is very much about being a servant leader. This means that leaders serve their teams rather than managing them. There are many different opinions about what Agile leaders look like, but here are some traits that are commonly valued in Agile leaders. Visionary. Adaptable. Flexible. Collaborative. Humble. Curious. Accepting change. Active Listener. Lifelong Learner. Self-aware. Ability to empower others. Lead by example. Natural Mentor. Positive Attitude. Courage to Take Risks. Critical Thinker. The Agile Leader's role is to use their own influence and time to get hurdles out of the way for the team so that they can do their best work.

An Agile leader coaches the team so that they can continuously improve the way they work and serves as a facilitator, creating events and interactions that build togetherness. The Agile Leader works hard to develop relationships within the team, across the organization and externally, so that the rest of the organization can support the team too. Individuals are supported with personal and interpersonal challenges and are trusted to get the job done. They feel empowered and appreciated by the people who lead them. In turn, this creates feelings of self efficacy, which makes them feel more motivated, productive, and part of something that matters. All managers are leaders, but leaders aren't always managers. Being a leader is not about having a position of authority.

You can become a leader simply by making the decision to be one. Leaders gain their influence through their actions and the way that they serve the people around them. They gain power through the respect others have for them, not because it was given to them by title. Agile leadership isn't about promoting a change to a new way of working. It is also about demonstrating the change that you want to see. You will inspire others when you lead by example, showing empathy and humility to your colleagues and striving to develop yourself. A good leader will never ask others to do a job that they wouldn't do themselves.

When you work this way, you'll be the leader that others want to follow. Even if you're not officially a manager. But you've got to walk the talk. If you say one thing but do another, you'll break the bonds of trust and credibility that you've worked so hard to build. Traditional managers are given positional power, and they expect their orders to be carried out even if their team doesn't trust or respect them. But hierarchy is much less important in agile organizations, so you need to build trust over time. Here are some tips for establishing yourself as a trustworthy leader. Tip number one: Get stuck in. A big part of leadership is the willingness to get your hands dirty and do the work. Tip number two, take responsibility.

When you make a mistake, say so. This shows humility and encourages others to do the same. Tip number three, tell the truth. If you don't know, it's okay to admit that. Be honest with your team. And they're more likely to be honest with you.

Tip number four Delegate freely. Encourage people to focus on their strengths and help them find ways to offload the tasks that drain them. Tip number five: Take calculated risks. Show that you are committed and can be trusted to follow through. Do what you say you will. Tip number six Acknowledge failure. This shows your team that failure is okay and even encouraged as part of the learning process. Tip number seven persists.

Show that your team won't be defined by its hurdles, but its creative solutions. Tip number eight Listen more than you talk. Ask questions and gather insights. Encourage dialogue. One person doesn't have to have all the answers, no matter how experienced they might be. Tip number nine Model Self Care. Show your team. It's good to take a break and find balance. Support others in doing the same. Tip number ten Value People show others that their well-being is important to you and the organization. Resolve conflict quickly and make a point of developing and supporting others. Tip number 11 Adapt your communication style. People have different preferences and like to be recognized in different ways. An Agile leader knows that there is no one good way to be a communicator. Instead, it's about matching the preferences of. Of the person or the group that you're working with. Tip number 12. Let go.

When something isn't working, try something else. Constantly challenge what you think you know and what you assume. Adapt to the moment before you move on to the next chapter. Take a moment to reflect on the traits of agile leaders that we identified. Which of these traits can you identify in yourself? Can you think of other traits not listed that you think are critical for an Agile leader? How could you work towards developing some of the traits that you don't have yet? There's some space for you to make notes in your Agile leadership plan. When you are finished, move on to the next chapter to try setting some leadership goals.

Setting Leadership Goals

We've talked about how having a purpose and feeling motivated are integral for teams working in an agile way. It's time to look for some motivators for your own team. Let's take a look at goal setting for a moment. An Agile leader sets strategic goals that are bold and inspirational. They push people to stretch and do things they have never done before. What if I said to you, your goal is to improve profitability by 35% in the next quarter through wearable device sales? Does that inspire you? Does that get you fired up? Do you want to tell your children about it? Probably not. But if I ask you to develop a wearable device that can indicate undiagnosed health conditions and save lives, well, now that's something, isn't it? It's a tougher goal to achieve potentially.

But if you can do it, you'll really be making a difference and you'll have learned a lot along the way. This is really where an Agile leader stands out. They help people to persist in pursuit of their shared goal, even when things get hard and the old ways of working want to take over. But before you move on to the next chapter, take a look at some goals that your team has at the moment. Can you reframe them to inspire the enthusiasm that you need to get people motivated? You may already be familiar with the concept of smart goals. These are specific, measured, attainable, realistic, time bound. So instead of saying My goal is to develop a strong and supportive agile team, your goal might instead be My goal is to develop an agile team of six people who use Agile principles to deliver a project with demonstrable cost and time savings of 30% when compared to a previous project.

Take a few moments to reframe three current goals in this way using your Agile leadership plan. Remember to think about what will motivate your team. How can you unite them behind a common vision and purpose? In this chapter we've explored the benefits of Agile and what Agile leadership looks like. You've benchmarked your own capabilities against this and we're starting to identify ways of developing yourself further. You also know how to set smart goals and have considered ways of motivating your team. Next in chapter three, we'll work on building your own self-awareness so that you can identify opportunities to improve your leadership capabilities. See you there.

Discovering Your Traits

You now know what Agile is and you can see its potential for your team on your way to becoming an Agile leader. You'll need to do a bit of self discovery. When you are self aware, you know what motivates you and what your strengths and weaknesses are. You also know what energizes and what drains you and where you may need to lean on others skills. We talked about being able to adjust your communication and leadership style based on who you are working with, but if you haven't put your energy into developing your own self awareness, you won't have a benchmark to work from. First, you'll need to know about your own personality as others see it. Of course, everyone has their own unique combination of traits, but there are various ways that we try to define personalities.

The Myers-Briggs type indicator is one that you're probably familiar with. It assesses personalities using these categories. Number one, introversion and extroversion. Number two, sensing versus intuition. Number three, thinking or feeling. Number four, judging or perception. If you've never taken a personality assessment, try it out in aid of your self awareness. There are lots of models out there, and none are perfect, Of course, but the act of working through a questionnaire will highlight some personality traits to guide your thinking. Even if your results aren't entirely scientific, the one we're going to work with is the ocean model, which evaluates your abilities by giving a high or low score across five different areas: openness, conscientiousness, extroversion, agreeableness and neuroticism.

It's also worth thinking specifically about leadership style when you do this. Tenenbaum and Schmidt identify four of these in their leadership continuum. On the left, we have the most autocratic style telling, and on the right, the more democratic style joining. Before you move on to the next chapter, let's try out a personality assessment. There are many personality assessments available online. Some are certainly more reliable than others. But if this is an aspect of yourself that you would like to explore more, try one out and see what your results are.

Here are a few options that you can find in the supporting document. 16 Personalities based on the MBti. The disk profile. The Big five. That's the ocean model. In your Agile leadership plan. Make some notes on how the experience of taking the assessment was for you and what you discovered about yourself. When you're ready, move on to the next step where you'll focus on your strengths.

Finding Your Strengths

The next part of self-awareness that is critical for leadership is understanding your own strengths. When you know what you are best at, you can focus on those areas and you'll know what to delegate or where to get support from others. You'll also do a better job of managing your weaknesses. When you know your own strengths, you'll also be more adept at identifying others strengths and nurturing those so that your team can shine. There are again, many different frameworks and tests available to help you reflect on your strengths via character strengths. And the High five tests are two options that you might like to try. Another way of discovering your strengths is to ask people who know you well to identify what they feel your strengths are.

Look for common traits when your feedback comes in and then list what this indicates about you. However you choose to zero in on your strengths once you have an idea of what these are. Spend some time reflecting on them. There's space for the notes in your Agile leadership plan. How have you used those strengths most recently? How can you use those strengths more at work so that you feel more fulfilled? When have you been in a role or project where you didn't use your strengths frequently? What was the impact? When you have completed your reflection, move on to the next chapter where we'll explore a concept that is critical for great leaders' emotional intelligence.

Persuasion And Influence

You've worked hard on your understanding of Agile and your self awareness so far. Now let's try out some actionable techniques for creating a successful, agile team and culture. Being persuasive and influential are critical skills for any leader. Since you're trying to demonstrate the appeal of a new way of working. You'll definitely need your skills of persuasion here. The Six Principles of Persuasion, as laid out by Robert Cialdini in his book Influence, are a helpful guide. Cialdini's six Principles are. Principle one Reciprocity. People are inclined to return the favor when you've done something for them. Principle two Social Proof. People look around to see how others respond while they work out how they will respond themselves.

Principle three Consistency. People want consistent commitments. Once they agree to something, they want to follow through. Principle four Likeability. People want to say yes to others who are like them and feel connected. Principle number five Authority. People want to follow the lead of experts. Principle number six, scarcity. People want something more if it's rare or it's exclusive. So what can you do to increase the perception of you across these areas? Well, reciprocity is fairly easy. Do a small favor or send a personal thank you note. That's about all it takes. If you consistently make an effort to help other people out, they'll be inclined to do the same for you.

Freely share your knowledge, publicly, praise others, and work to build up some social obligations that people want to return to you. Each of these favors will be returned to you at some point to your advantage. But don't go overboard with it. If you aren't genuine, it will be obvious. What about social proof? Humans are social animals, after all, and we usually want to conform to social norms when making decisions or showing our support. We look around to see what everyone else is doing first. So when you introduce an idea or change that you want people to buy into, show them that your idea has support from others.

Are other departments in the organization championing the cause? Can you show evidence that what you are suggesting has worked well in similar organizations? Maybe there's a testimonial or a guest speaker that can provide the social boost you're looking for. Next, we've got consistency. People like to be consistent with their self image. If a colleague publicly commits to your project, they are much more likely to do what they've said they would because they want to be seen as reliable. Similarly, you can use the principle of consistency to get people to agree to small things first so that when you introduce gradually bigger tasks, they don't feel like it's such a leap. For example, let's say you change one small thing about how your team works, like introducing a new tech tool.

From there you might introduce another small tool and another until you have an entirely new system working. Next is likeability. We are more influenced by people that we like than people that we don't like. And who are the people that we find likable? We like people who are similar to us, who pay us compliments and cooperate with us. Human nature is quite simple, really. Using mirroring techniques, complementing each other, making people smile. That's what likeability is about. But again, if you try too hard to get people to like you or your approach feels disingenuous, you might have the opposite effect. Cialdini's next principle is authority. Essentially, people respect authority and want to follow the lead of experts.

So demonstrate your expertise and credentials to help people trust you. Of course, this is another principle where you need to be quite careful about your approach. If you're boastful, people will find that quite unlikable. It's far better when other people can vouch for you, particularly if those people have an element of authority themselves. Finally we have scarcity. The more exclusive something is, the more we want it. This one is used all the time in marketing. Only five seats left at this Price Limited edition. The sale ends on Friday. Being part of a selective team leading the way to bring an Agile organization across the line.

Sounds like something people want to be a part of. Chances are you can get people on side by offering them the opportunity to be part of something innovative and exclusive. Using the scarcity principle to your advantage. Before you move on to the next chapter, make some notes in your Agile leadership plan about how you can more effectively use Cialdini's six Principles to Build Your influence. Try to identify at least one habit or action for each of these principles. When you're ready, move on to the next chapter where we'll explore a word that leaders are usually keen to avoid conflict.

Handling Conflict

Conflict is unavoidable on any team, but even more so on Agile teams where team members depend on each other for performance. So as an Agile leader, you'll need to know how to navigate conflict. Now you might think, well, if a conflict doesn't happen in the first place, we won't have anything to worry about. That's a worthy goal. But it's unrealistic to think that a group of people working as closely together as your Agile team will never disagree. A level of conflict can be healthy. It means that people care about what they do enough to get fired up about it. Having passionate people on your team is no bad thing. But how can you make sure that conflict doesn't get out of hand or affect the team's overall performance? Well, give them a life raft. This is a model developed by Speed Lees in 1985.

It gives us five escalating levels of conflict to look out for. These are level one, a problem to solve. Level two Disagreement. Level three Conflict. Level four. Crusade. Level five. World War. So let's go to level one. A problem to solve. Here we are at the level of everyday conflict, your typical misunderstanding, difference of opinion and contrasting goals. These little niggles happen all the time, but just because they are minor doesn't mean we can ignore them. Conflict in the air can change the dynamic within the team and create anxiety, which in turn means they aren't working at their best. When you've got a conflict at this level, get together with the team and figure it out. What's wrong and how can we fix it? Share information freely.

Be clear and specific, but stick to the facts and the present moment. This isn't the place for dredging up the past. Check in with each other and work out what miscommunication has happened. There shouldn't be an emotional conversation, simply a way to collaborate on finding a constructive way forward. Here, your role as a leader is to make sure that every team member is heard and respected. Guide them towards a win-win situation. They need a little nudge towards finding a solution that works for everyone. Then we have level two disagreement. At this level, people start to distance themselves from each other so that they can protect themselves. There may be some behind the scenes conversations happening where people are looking for advice and support.

Things can get a little heated here with the team's usual sense of humor becoming a little bit more sarcastic and weary. People speak more generally and don't share everything that they know. There's a lot of interpretation and misinterpretation going on. Usually the people experiencing the conflict will wait for someone to intervene. So this is where you come in. Bring the team together and open a discussion aiming to help them resolve the disagreement themselves. Reminding them of their shared values. There is a willingness to discuss and fix the problem, but the team will probably not come together on their own. So you will need to create an opportunity for them to work it out.

Now we come to level three context. At this level, lingering conflicts and problems that have gone unresolved start to compound and become bigger issues. There can be some warring for power here. People start to take sides and emotional arguments sway their teammates to one side or another. People and problems become one and the same and personal attacks begin to happen. Overgeneralizations such as you always did this and you never listen are really common. People will resist moving beyond blame. So your role is to get the team to stick to the facts and do some negotiating. Help them to recognize that their relationships with each other are more important than the issue.

Get the discussion going and make sure that personal rivalries are put aside for the good of the team. At level four, people believe that the other side won't change. There may be a feeling that the only option is to leave the team or remove someone else. The sides become pitted against each other and the team begins to split. People become under attack based on what side they are on rather than their ideas. We're arguing over principles here rather than facts and specific issues. Attitudes are spiteful with each side believing they are better than the other. You might not be able to get both sides together for a discussion, so facilitate and de-escalate the conflict to a lower level where you can guide them towards a solution.

You will likely need to speak to each side separately and then try to resolve the differences. Calming things down well before bringing them both to the table to discuss. Finally, we come to level five World War. At this level, the situation is very combative. Each side wants to destroy the other to win. The other must lose. A constructive outcome is unlikely. So as a leader, you will need to separate the people who are fighting and try to limit the damage to the team more widely. Hopefully you won't find yourself here often or at all, but if you do, you've found an unresolvable conflict and you need to find a way for everyone to continue working together without hurting each other.

Remember a little bit of conflict at levels one and two isn't such a bad thing. It indicates that your team members are motivated and invested in what they're working on. But when you start to reach the upper levels of the conflict scale, things get unproductive and this can have damaging effects on the team. So though your instinct might be to ignore or avoid conflict, get some practice in facilitating conflict resolution, work on creating an open, supportive environment that doesn't allow conflict to expand. In the next chapter, we'll take a look at how to nurture an Agile culture.

Cultural Agility

You'll find that a small team of 5 to 8 members is ideal for an Agile team. Any more than this and things get complicated. There will be more emails and meetings and all sorts of things that an Agile team wants to minimize to keep their productivity up on a small team. It is easier to build trust. The group works with each other every day and are in frequent communication with each other. With a small group, we also have more room to experiment and sometimes fail without worrying about being judged. Employees in small teams are also more likely to voice their own opinions and challenge each other so they can make better, more thought out decisions and avoid groupthink.

But though keeping your agile team small might be your goal, there are inevitably people outside of this small group who have some influence over how it operates. Let's talk about organizational influence. Your team may be agile or on its way to becoming so, but you may be working within a larger organization that isn't as agile as you would like it to be. There will be things that you need that are outside of your Agile team's scope, so you'll need to engage with non agile teams like payroll, legal or investor relations. Part of your job as a leader is to help the organization optimize for flexibility and continuous improvement, ensuring that the focus is always on the customer and that other parts of the organization support that mission, even if they don't work the same way that your team does. Let's talk about fostering an agile culture.

One of the most important things you can do when leading with agility is create a culture that makes learning a priority. Your team should be always looking to make the customer experience better. The challenge for you, though, is that you can't dictate the culture. You can only create the conditions to help to form it. Most of a team's culture comes from how people treat each other and work together, so you can't control it directly, but you can set examples and model behaviors that will help your team create this naturally for themselves. When you are in the early stages of bringing an Agile team together, here are some factors to look for in team members.

Number one. Team players who recognize that their actions have an impact on others. Number two, an attitude that focuses on we rather than I. Number three, people who you can trust to take ownership of their tasks and manage their own workload. Number four, versatile people with T-shaped skills. They have expert knowledge in a particular area and enough knowledge about various other areas that they can collaborate with other disciplines. There isn't a formula for the perfect agile team. Some use the Scrum framework, other teams use Kanban, a system of visualizing tasks based on whether they are requested in progress or done with each team member picking up a new task as their capacity allows.

Ideally, agile teams are co-located, but team members could work remotely from different locations in practice. Usually an Agile team would have all of the skills needed to complete a project within its team. Members aim for that and be open to getting specialists involved on an ad hoc basis if you need to. In the next chapter, we will take a look at how to design your ideal agile team.

Designing An Agile Dream Team

You may be working with an existing team, expanding your team, or beginning your agile journey at the point of hiring. No matter what your starting point is, Tuckman's stages of group development are a useful way of understanding what a team will go through as it grows. Team development is a cycle. The performing stage is where great development work happens. In this phase, you have a robust and collaborative team that works very well together, but the cycle starts over more often than you might expect. Your team could be happily speeding along in the performing stages and then bring a new person on board. Back to forming we go. Or let's say the company strategy changes. That could send you back to the storming phases.

Don't worry, when the team shifts back a phase or two, it doesn't mean that there's anything wrong with your leadership. It's simply that when a change happens, teams need a moment to steady themselves. There is another element of high performing agile teams that you should try to build into your own. Knowledge sharing. You can give team members lots of opportunities to learn from each other through mentoring and sharing skill sets. If only one person on a team has a particular skill set, they'll become a single point of failure if they are ill or if they leave the team. So by encouraging skill sharing, you can protect the team against these possibilities. Let's discuss six conditions for high performing teams. Research from Harvard University has identified six conditions for effective teams.

Their framework identifies six conditions that can be designed into a team. Together, these conditions account for up to 80% of a team's effectiveness. Three essentials identified are. Condition one The right people with the range of skills and perspectives needed to do the work. Condition two A real team, A clearly identified team that are together long enough to accomplish a meaningful result. Condition number three A compelling purpose. The commitment to work towards a shared goal. The three enablers identified are, number one, a sound structure, clear norms around how the team will work together. Number two, a supportive context. The broader networks and systems promote teamwork and remove obstacles. Number three, team coaching.

An excellent coach can help the team make the best use of its resources. Before you move on to the next chapter, use the six Conditions framework to think about the ideal makeup of your team. Are each of the six conditions met? If they aren't, what changes are needed to make that possible? Make some notes in your leadership plan about this in chapter four. You've been developing ideas about how you can persuade and influence others, handle conflict, foster an agile culture, and design an Agile team. Your next step is to commit to some goals and actions based on what you've learned to take your Agile leadership capabilities to the next level. When you are ready to make a commitment to your leadership development, move on to chapter five. I'll see you there.

Introducing Agile To An Existing Team

If you are working with a team that's used to a more hierarchical way of organizing, Agile may be a new concept to them. So you'll need to get buy-in by showing them why you want to adopt agile processes and how it will help them. If you do present this as an opportunity for them to grow their own skill sets and become part of an innovative process. Some people have only heard about Agile in the context of IT and software development projects, so you may need to present it instead as a method for improving productivity and well being. There is some upfront chapter to be done to help the team understand how agile processes work.

You might want to introduce Scrum and set up daily stand ups, retrospectives and other events to keep things moving. Or you may want to adopt a slightly different approach. The important thing is that the approach is communicated to everyone clearly and consistently. a chapter isn't something that you do once, even if your team has a good grasp of agile concepts as you introduce them, they may forget some of the best practices over time. So hold regular sessions to reinforce and build new skills. Leaders too, need to be constantly learning. The more you know, the more effort you put into your own development, the better off your team will be.

Team members are probably used to taking commands from a manager, but as an Agile team, their allegiance is to each other rather than to the manager. This can take some getting used to, but it is something that you can all get better at with practice and frequent communication with each other. You'll also need to set up some tools to help your team visualize and manage their workload. Many agile teams use a Kanban board to see what's in the backlog yet to be assigned, which tasks are in progress and which are done. This way each person can accept new work when they can. The most seamless way to induct Agile is to apply it to a project that your team is currently working on. Here's one way that you could approach this. Decide if you'll use Scrum Kanban or another Agile methodology.

Scrum is a well known Agile project management methodology. It uses time bound sprints of work, usually around two weeks long. Scrum includes four events that make up each sprint. These are Sprint planning meetings. The team decides what work from the backlog will be included in the sprint. Only the team can add work to the sprint. Then we have the sprint demo. The team showcases the work they have done in the current iteration. You have the daily stand up, a 15 minute meeting each day where the team discusses progress and roadblocks. And then you have a retrospective. The team reviews the results of the previous sprint and tweaks their progress based on what they have learned.

Kanban is an agile methodology built on continuous delivery which tries hard not to overburden the team. Instead of using tightly time bound sprints, Kanban teams organize around a limited number of work in progress tasks and can release an iteration of work at any time when they're ready. There are a few elements that make Kanban unique. Number one, visualize the workflow with a Kanban board. Kanban uses a visual board to keep track of progress. Number two limit work in progress teams set a limit on how many tasks may be in progress at any time. Number three: Release when the team is ready. Rather than releasing an increment of work at the end of a scrum Kanban teams can release work when they are prepared to hold a planning meeting to define the project scope.

Get buy-in from stakeholders and define the need that the project is addressing. The team will be flexible and adapt based on feedback, but you should still have a clear idea of what the project is trying to do before you begin. Let's talk about creating a roadmap. The strategy has been defined in the project planning meeting, but now you need a roadmap for the project. This is your big picture view. Work out what the requirements are and what the timeframe looks like. You don't have to put dates next to every step of the project, but it does help to make a rough estimate about the effort and the time each of the main goals will require. For each project's goals, try to include a rough date and the key features that the team needs to create the metrics you'll use to measure the goals completion.

Agile is about moving quickly rather than doing a lot of planning upfront, so don't get too bogged down in the details at this point. You need enough detail to know what it will take to get your minimum viable product MVP. Now let's move on to planning your sprint. How long will it be? And what are the tasks and goals that the team is focusing on? The team will create a list of backlog items that you can aim to complete in the sprint. Now it's time to get to work. Agile projects move quickly, so get the team going on their tasks now. You might decide to have daily stand ups to check in with each other. These meetings are just 15 minutes long if you include them in your process.

Each person should come to the stand up and answer What did you do yesterday? What are you working on today? Is there anything in your way? Then we need to review your sprint. When you finish your sprint and release a piece of work, it's time to celebrate and show off what you've done. A bit like show and tell. Bring the team and the stakeholders together to do this. This is an opportunity to make sure all the requirements were met according to the team's definition of done and the product owner's satisfaction. Then you need to check in on how you did. Now that you've shown off your work, check in as a team and decide what we learned? How can we do better in the next sprint? This retrospective can happen right after your review.

Create a short list of improvements and changes that the team wants to implement in the next sprint. So what's next from here? Start over its back to the sprint planning meeting as your next sprint should start right after the previous one ends. Pat yourself on the back but also keep the momentum up until the project is complete. In your Agile leadership plan, outline how you will introduce Agile to your team. You may need to do some light research to find out more about Scrum or Kanban or other agile frameworks. And when you've completed this task, move on to the next chapter to find out about how collaboration might look on your Agile team.

Collaboration

If you are trying to put an Agile team together in an organization that is traditional and siloed, it can be tricky to break out of this prevailing culture. To enable successful collaboration on your Agile team, your tasks as a leader are to clearly define roles, communicate openly with your teams, get consensus on goals and processes, and respect everyone's contribution no matter their role or seniority. Identify obstacles and work hard to get them out of your team's way. Hold the best interests of your team higher than personal goals or political gains. Acknowledge mistakes and failures. Learn and then move on. Effective collaboration begins with trust, but it's not as easy as it sounds to achieve this.

When you enforce collaboration or it is implemented ineffectively, that can be worse than no collaboration at all. Collaboration is no magic bullet. For example, if people are too busy networking to get anything done, collaboration isn't giving you the results you're looking for. So look for opportunities for collaboration, spot barriers and tailor the collaboration opportunities to the team and the project. Next, we'll take a look at a related issue: how you enable team members to take ownership of their work and their decisions.

Enabling Others

As you know, agile teams aren't hierarchical. They are small and highly collaborative. Having a close knit team is critical for success. So a big part of the leadership role is empowering others by giving them the freedom, flexibility and power to make decisions and solve problems. In a traditional organization, decisions are made by upper management and cascaded down. But this is an authoritative way to lead. It is time consuming, and the bureaucracy it creates means that an organization isn't as quick to react to changing conditions as its agile counterparts are. So to make Agile work, teams need to be able to clear hurdles for themselves. They need to be accountable for their decisions, Of course, but they must be self-organizing for Agile to be successful.

This autonomy makes people feel energized, capable and determined. It makes a big difference to employee well-being, job satisfaction and productivity. And as a bonus, it saves time and reduces costs. It makes sense that the people doing the work are the ones to make decisions about it. They are the closest to it. They know what needs to be done. So often the best thing a leader can do is to get out of their way and let them do it. In return, you'll get an increased dedication and loyalty. You need to look at the three critical elements so that your team feels engaged and empowered. Number one, a positive relationship with their direct manager. Number two, confidence in the senior leadership.

Number three, pride in working for the organization. If employees don't have a good relationship with their line manager, they won't feel comfortable with their place on the team. You want this line of communication to be open and honest? Facilitate a positive relationship by having regular check ins and making sure that the line manager is responsive. When the employee needs help, they need to know that the manager is looking out for them. Without this relationship, the employee won't likely stick around for very long. Teams have got to be confident that they know where the company is headed and want to be part of that vision. Here, organizations can fall down when they don't do an excellent job of communicating strategy to their employees.

In many cases, employees can feel out of the loop in terms of what upper management is doing. But this goes against the openness needed to make Agile work. Finally, people need to feel like what they do matters. Can they go home and feel good about how they spend so much of their time when the company is making a positive contribution and the employee feels confident about their part in the bigger picture? They will feel engaged and empowered by what they do. So how can you enable your team to do the best work? Here are some tips. Number one, open up communication. Give your team structured ways of making their observations and feelings known.

This might be through retrospectives and brainstorming sessions, shared notice boards in one to ones and wherever else you can make sure they know that their input is valued even if you go another way. Acknowledge them for sharing and reward their input. That helps the company. Number two rewards self-improvement. Help your people to grow. Put aside some time and some money for the personal development chapter. Help people to create plans for their growth and reward them for their achievements. This way, they'll happily apply their new skills to help the team. Number three makes failure an option. People are usually risk averse, especially when it comes to the workplace.

But if your team feels like they are constantly having to justify their decisions, get approval before they act or apologize for failure, they won't have a chance to innovate. Give people a chance to try new things. Set up experiments and checkpoints so that there is room to test ideas and learn from failures and successes. Number four, give them context. You may be privy to a lot of information that your teammates don't know about yet. They are expected to take action as if they knew everything that you do. Share what you know with them consistently. When employees understand where things are going, they can make better decisions. Number five Define roles. People need to know what they are supposed to do and where their boundaries are so that they're not duplicating efforts or stepping on toes.

You'll need to be clear about what each person is there to do and suggest ways of cooperating to get the best out of everyone. Number six: Make them accountable. Don't leave your team guessing about whether they are doing things right or not. Measure progress openly. So not only do individual employees know that they're meeting expectations, but also that others are being held accountable, too. This is a big part of motivating your team. Number seven, give them independence. Agile is not about micromanaging, so leave that well behind. Give people the opportunity to do their own thing and you will be pleasantly surprised by what they learn and how they grow. Number eight: Appreciate them. Sure.

That paycheck at the end of the month is a reward, but your best people aren't there just because they're getting paid. They want to feel satisfied and appreciated. So say thank you and celebrate small wins at every opportunity before you move on to the next chapter. Make some notes in your Agile leadership plan about actions you can take to improve team members' relationships with their direct manager. Confidence in the senior leadership and pride in working for the organization. Could you incorporate any of the tips suggested, or can you think of other ways to make the team feel enabled and in control of their work environment? There is some space to make notes in your Agile leadership plan. When you've done this, move on to the next chapter where you'll develop your 90 day Agile leadership plan.

Your 90-day Agile Leadership Plan

You are nearly there. Well done for making it through this Book. Now that you have reflected on your leadership skills and looked around you at your team and the organization you're working in, you should have a good idea of the opportunities and potential barriers that lie ahead as you work towards agility. Now it's time to make some commitments. First, make sure you have completed the exercises we've set out for you in the Agile Leadership Plan document. So far, the reflections you've done will contribute to the commitments you make now, so you might like to skim through your responses. You will find a chapter titled Your 90 day Agile Leadership Plan towards the end of the document.

This is where you will commit to a goal for each of the next 30, 60 and 90 days. First, capture the most critical issues that you have discovered so far. Start with yourself. What are the skills you want to develop to improve your leadership agility and how will you do so? What habits or practices have you identified that you want to change or stop doing, and how could you approach that? Next, you'll consider the team. What skills and capabilities have you identified that your team will need to increase its agility and how could you access those? Then the big picture: What are the most impactful barriers at the organizational level and what are some ways that you could overcome those? Finally, use the details you have captured to create three smart goals.

You have some space in your plan to identify actions for each one. Try to break these down into small, achievable tasks that you can check off one by one. Any resources or support you need to achieve your goal. Here you might capture things like time, equipment, people or funds. We've set you three time frames: 30 days, 60 days and 90 days. So decide which goal fits each time frame best. You may find that your personal goals are better fit for the shorter time frame because you have more influence in this area, but that you need the 90 day time frame to implement actions at an organizational level.

Refer back to your plan frequently over the coming months to make sure that you are on track towards your goals. Check off each action as you complete it. Once the 90 day term has passed, take a look to make sure that you have achieved the three goals you set for yourself and make a point to celebrate what you have achieved. But it doesn't have to stop there. There is no perfect leader. Your work here is ongoing. You can use this goal setting method to build a continuous improvement cycle for yourself and your team.

Recap

Congratulations for making it to the end of this Book. Throughout the last few chapters, you've explored the traits and habits that make for a great Agile leader, and you've discovered the benefits of this way of working for teams and organizations more widely. We've briefly looked at Agile as a project management methodology, and you now know that you can use it alongside other frameworks like Scrum or Kanban to run projects with your team. In this approach you would use short sprints of work, frequent delivery of working products and events like team retrospectives to build a culture of continuous learning and improvement while also becoming better at communicating and being transparent with each other within the team.

Perhaps more importantly, though, we've looked at Agile as a mindset, an approach to work that encompasses more than just how you manage projects. You now know about the skills and capabilities that an Agile leader needs, from flexibility to humility and critical thinking to calculated risk taking. You've worked hard to develop your self-awareness during this Book, taking time to look at your own personality traits and strengths, to find out where you are now and where you have room to improve. Not only have you discovered ways of improving your own agility as a leader, but you've also developed ideas about how you can influence others, deal with conflict and foster an agile culture. When you implement these ideas using the leadership plan that you've designed.

You'll find that agility comes easier to your team. You can help nudge your organization into an agile direction more widely because you'll have the successful implementation on your team as a shining example of how well Agile could work across the whole organization. There will still be some challenges to overcome, Of course, but you have done a lot of the hard work here by accepting your role as the driver of your team's agile journey. Now it's time to put what you've learned into practice and in the process create a happier, healthier and more productive environment to work in. Thank you so much for joining us on this learning journey.

We have a whole catalog Of courses available, so be sure to check out the categories and topics relevant to you and your organization's best wishes from the Expert Academy. And good luck.

Agile Business Processes

Welcome to the Book on Agile business processes. If you're looking to expand your knowledge of the Agile methodology to optimize your project management process or you want to learn how to budget for Agile projects, this Book is going to help you. It will also provide tips on getting full buy-in from every member of your team when transitioning to Agile ways of working and boosting team engagement overall. This Book is going to take your application of Agile to a new level, helping you to solve common challenges that arise along with this way of working. First, we'll recap on the fundamentals of Agile. Then we'll cover the following topics. Agile Budgeting Processes. Common challenges in the Agile methodology and How to overcome them.

How to align agile working styles with individual needs, including the needs of Neurodivergent individuals. How to use the Agile methodology as an opportunity to boost engagement and more. So let's begin. The Agile methodology started in 2001 as a popular software development methodology, which was later adopted for use in business projects across industries. According to data from 2021 published by business management consulting company J-curve, developing a strong agile culture within an organization increases commercial performance by 237%, and 70% of Agile organizations say that the method helps them attain a faster time to market. With that in mind, it's no wonder that Agile is used by 71% of companies in the US.

The Agile methodology is based on a set of values and principles that emphasize collaboration, feedback and adaptive planning. Unlike traditional project management approaches, Agile is focused on delivering results quickly and efficiently while still maintaining high quality standards. This gives Agile many advantages, including the following. Number one rapid response to change. This is why Agile is well suited to the software development process. And with the pace of change in today's world, this flexibility is needed in a diverse range of business scenarios. If something unexpected comes up or if the scope of the project changes, it's easy to make adjustments without having to start from scratch.

Number two: Improved communication. Agile promotes transparency and communication among team members. This can help to prevent misunderstandings and conflict and ensure that everyone is working towards the same goal. Number three. Cost savings. This benefit is vital when it comes to software development. Software projects have always been notorious for going over budget. This is partly because older methodologies that were in place before Agile was invented, such as the waterfall method, involve such a linear approach to development. There is not much flexibility or iteration, meaning that if there are any changes or problems with the project, it's very difficult and costly to fix them.

In addition, the waterfall method often leads to unrealistic expectations about the project timeline, which can again result in cost overruns. In fact, according to research in 2018 from Software Development Advisory Organization, the Standish Group, Agile projects are twice as likely to succeed compared to projects that use the Waterfall method. Now let's review some of the key practices that are essential for success in applying the Agile methodology. Number one, having a strong team backbone. This means that the team has members who are skilled in agile and can help guide and support other team members through the process. Number two. Delivering value to the customer.

This means that teams should always be thinking about how they can add value to the product or service they are working with. They should also be constantly seeking feedback from customers so they can make improvements. Number three. Embracing change in Agile development. Change is a constant and teams need to be able to adapt to it. They should be open to new ideas and willing to experiment. Number for short iterations. Short iterations are a hallmark of the Agile methodology. This means that work is done in short cycles, known as sprints, which allows for rapid response to change.

This also allows for constant feedback from stakeholders, which is essential for making sure that the project is on track. Number five Communication. Communication is key in any project, but it is especially important in agile development. This is because the Agile methodology relies on constant feedback in order to be successful. All team members should be aware of the project's goals and progress and they should feel comfortable raising any concerns that they have. And number six, reviewing and improving processes. It's important to constantly review and improve processes. This is because the Agile methodology is based on the principle of continuous improvement.

By constantly reviewing and improving processes, teams can ensure that they are always working in the most efficient way possible. Following these key practices will help your team be successful with Agile development. And with that, we've reached the end of this introductory chapter. Your task is to download and complete the introduction worksheet. After that, join me in the next chapter where we'll run through all the important concepts and key terms from the Agile methodology. If you've worked with Agile before, this will provide a helpful recap. If Agile is new for you, it will give you a detailed overview of everything you need to know to get started. So complete the worksheet, then join me in the next chapter.

Key Concepts In Agile

Welcome to chapter two. Here, we'll run through all the important concepts you need to be aware of when working with Agile processes. We've also included some terms that are specific to software development. But if you don't work in this field, you don't need to worry about those. So let's begin. First, we'll start with the different types of meetings that occur in Agile projects. Number one kickoff meeting. A kickoff meeting is a meeting held at the start of a project to discuss the goals and objectives of the project, as well as to ensure that everyone is on the same page. Number two, stand up meetings in a short daily meeting, typically 15 minutes or less, in which team members discuss what they did yesterday, what they planned to do today, and any impediments to their progress.

Stand up meetings help keep teams focused and on track. Number three retrospective A meeting held at the end of each sprint in which team members reflect on what went well and what could have been improved. Retrospectives help teams learn from their experiences and continuously improve their process. Next, we'll look at a few concepts regarding the structure of Agile processes. Number one Scrum is a framework for managing work on complex projects. Scrum is characterized by short development cycles called sprints, which allow teams to rapidly develop and deliver new features.

Number two, Sprint, as we just mentioned. A sprint is a fixed length iteration of work, typically two weeks during which a team produces a deliverable for a specific milestone. Sprints are a key component of the Scrum framework and allow teams to work at a sustainable pace while still delivering value rapidly. Number three Sprint Goal. A short term goal that a team sets at the beginning of each sprint. Sprint goals help keep teams focused on delivering value to the customer. Number four product backlog, a prioritized list of features or work items that a team plans to implement in future sprints. Number five.

Sprint backlog. A list of work items that a team plans to implement in the current sprint. The sprint backlog is created at the beginning of each sprint and is refined throughout the sprint as new information about the work is discovered. Number six Burndown Chart. A graphical representation of the amount of work remaining to be done in a sprint. Burndown charts help teams track their progress and identify potential problems early. Number seven Stack rank A method of prioritizing work items in which items are ranked from most to least important. Stack ranking helps ensure that the most important work items are completed first. Number eight Velocity.

A measure of the amount of work that a team can complete in a given period of time, typically one sprint. Velocity is used to predict how much work the team can complete in future sprints and to identify trends in the team's performance. Now let's look at the different roles in an Agile team. Number one product owner, the person responsible for prioritizing the work in the product backlog and ensuring that the team is delivering value to the customer. The product owner is typically a member of the product development team. Number two. Scrum Master. The person responsible for facilitating the scrum process and ensuring that the team is following the Scrum rules in software projects.

The Scrum Master is typically a member of the development team. Number three Agile coach. A person who helps a team transition to and adopt an agile development methodology. Agile coaches provide guidance and support to teams as they learn how to work in an agile way. Now for some concepts and tools that facilitate the Agile working process and help teams to recognize when they've reached their objectives. Number one Taskboard. A physical or virtual board that displays the tasks to be completed in a sprint. Task boards help teams track their progress, balance workloads and identify bottlenecks. Number two user stories.

A way of describing how a unit of work will deliver value to the customer. For example, the user story of a learning and development specialist may be that I want to assess my employees' chapter needs so that I can plan the correct chapter sessions. User stories help us understand the requirements of different stakeholders in order to design solutions that cater to those needs. In software development, user stories relate to the specific functionality that each type of user would need to have access to. For example, as a customer service representative, I need to have access to customer records so that I can resolve their issues. Number three, acceptance criteria. A set of conditions that must be met in order for a user story to be considered done.

Acceptance criteria are usually specific and measurable, and they help ensure that user stories are testable. Number four definition of done. A set of criteria that must be met before a work item can be considered complete. The definition of done helps ensure that all work items are of high quality and meet the customer's requirements. The next set of Agile terms relates specifically to software development. If you don't work with software projects, you won't need to remember these terms. Number one test driven development. A software development methodology in which tests are written before code is written. Test driven development helps ensure that code is of high quality and that it meets the requirements of the test.

Number two pair programming, a method of software development in which two programmers work together at one computer with one person writing code and the other person reviewing it. Pair programming helps to ensure that code is of high quality and that both programmers have a shared understanding of the code. Number three, Continuous integration. A practice where changes to the code are integrated into the main codebase frequently, typically multiple times per day. Continuous integration helps reduce the risk of merge conflicts and ensures that all team members are working with the most up to date code. Number for continuous delivery, a practice where software is released to production frequently.

Typically multiple times per day. Continuous delivery helps reduce the risk of bugs and ensures that customers always have the latest version of the software. Okay. That was quite a lot to take in. Before we end the chapter, there is one more concept from Agile software development to discuss Planning poker. Planning Poker, also known as Scrum Poker, is a gamified technique for estimating mostly used to estimate the required effort in software engineering. In planning, poker, team members make estimates by placing cards face down on the table instead of voicing their opinion directly. After everyone shows their cards and discusses the estimates by hiding the estimates until they are all revealed.

Planning poker avoids the influence of anchoring, where the first numbers spoken aloud makes others lean towards giving a similar figure. Common sense would dictate that the larger and more complex a user story is, the more time it will take to complete. While this may be true in some cases, there are often other factors that need to be considered when estimating user stories. These can include. The team's experience level. The complexity of the technology being used. The novelty of the feature and how well understood the requirements are. Planning. Poker is just one tool that can be used to help arrive at an estimate for a user story.

When combined with other estimation techniques, it can provide a more accurate picture of the effort required to complete a user story. You've now reached the end of chapter two. Your task is to download and complete the User Stories worksheet. After that, join me in chapter three where we'll cover Agile budgeting techniques.

Agile Budgeting

Welcome to chapter three, where you'll learn about some agile budgeting techniques. Agile budgeting can be a challenge for organizations because it requires a different approach to allocating and managing finances. In traditional budgeting, funds are typically allotted up front for specific projects or activities. Agile budgeting, on the other hand, relies on a more flexible approach. Agile budgeting may also require organizations to reallocate funds from one area to another as priorities shift over time as a result. Effective agile budgeting requires careful planning and coordination between different teams and departments. A common way to budget for agile projects is to calculate the cost per iteration or sprint.

Before we review the best practices for doing that, we will review Agile pricing. Agile pricing is based on two things: time and materials. Time is self-explanatory. It's the amount of time your team will spend working on the project. Materials, on the other hand, are the costs of things like tools, software, hardware and other equipment, chapter, transport or any other resources that your team will need to complete the project. To calculate the cost per iteration, take the daily rate for each team member and multiply that by the percentage of the time converted into decimals that they will be working on the project. So if they will be working 50% of the time, you would multiply it by 0.5. Then multiply the result by the number of days allocated to the iteration.

Do the same for all members of the team to get the total cost for time. Next, calculate the cost of materials and add that to the budget. In Agile projects, contingency costs are factored into the budget and this is usually at a rate of 10 to 50% of the total cost, not including contingency costs risks the following happening the project going over budget or unable to be completed. The project deadline is getting pushed back, losing trust from investors and other stakeholders. As you can tell, it's vital to include a good amount of funding to prevent any of these things from happening.

So how should you calculate the contingency budget? It's all based on calculating what is known as the confidence level. How confident you are that the assigned budget is going to allow you to get the job done. This is also known as the confidence interval. There are different ways to determine the confidence level in some teams, the project manager and other experts will each state a percentage regarding how confident they are about the likelihood of the budget being sufficient. This is based on the requirements as well as risks in complex projects. Various risk assessment data may factor into the equation. We will look more at risk assessment in a moment.

So once each relevant stakeholder has voted, an average percentage will then be calculated weighted. Based on that percentage, you can calculate the contingency budget. You multiply the base rate of the project or iteration by the chosen contingency percentage. The percentage for contingency, as we mentioned, is usually between 10 to 50%. And the higher the confidence level, the lower the percentage will be. A very high confidence level may therefore require only 10% contingency.

Therefore, if the cost for one sprint was £20,000, 10% of that total budget is £2,000. So the total budget per sprint would be £22,000. The cost per sprint may not be completely accurate in the beginning, but after several iterations and a bit of tweaking, the budget is usually reliable.

However, if the budget changes significantly from the original estimate, the scope of the project may change. If the budget turns out to be considerably more than expected, it's possible that the project will end once a minimum viable product is ready rather than something more polished. On the other hand, if investment increases at any stage, the budget may be updated to allow for further work to be done when the cost per sprint is based on a fixed price quote and not time and materials, you simply take the total estimated cost of the project and divide it by the number of sprints, then add in the required contingency amount. Also note that in fixed price projects the scope will be variable.

After reviewing the progress for each sprint, it's possible that features will be reprioritized or removed. Now back to risk assessment. Some risks that may affect Agile projects include. Team members being assigned to multiple projects. Misunderstanding of requirements. Third parties not delivering required products or services on time, team members being off sick or taking annual leave. Team members not being as skilled as expected. Delays in approvals from key stakeholders and unexpected events or emergencies. All of these risks can contribute to delays, budget overruns or both. To start forming risk mitigation and contingency plans, you need to prioritize each risk and decide what type of action it requires.

To prioritize risks, you need to calculate the risk rating. First determine which risks would be the most impactful, also known as the risk severity and which would be the most likely. The severity of impact is rated on a scale from 1 to 5. You then rate the likelihood of the risk occurring and record this as a percentage. Next, multiply the risk severity by the probability and that gives you the risk rating. You can then decide whether a risk has a high enough rating and is therefore a big enough threat to require some type of mitigative action or whether there is no action required. Typically when four Books of action are assigned to each risk. Risk avoidance. Eliminating the cause of the risk mitigation.

Minimizing the consequences of a risk by lowering its severity or likelihood of occurring. Acceptance. Accepting the risk if it occurs. In other words, taking no preventative action. And finally, transference, such as assigning the risk to an insurance company. Assessing risks in this way will help you gain more clarity about the confidence level to assign to the project so you can get an accurate idea about the contingency budget. In Agile project management, the risk of delays and budget overruns are often assessed using a technique called Monte Carlo simulations. This technique involves using statistical models to generate multiple possible outcomes for a given situation and the probability of each of those outcomes occurring from there.

Risk mitigation methods can be put into place. Suppose you estimate that your project will be complete within six months. If everything goes according to plan, a Monte Carlo simulation will be able to tell you by how much your project may be delayed depending on how the project deviates from the plan. For example, suppose there was a minor delay in a third party completing part of the work. The results of the simulation will show a probability distribution along the lines of the following probability of completing the project in six months. 90% probability of completing the project in eight months. 100% probability of completing the project in ten months.

50% probability of completing the project in 12 months. 30%. When calculating risk using Monte Carlo simulations, it is important to remember that the results are only as good as the historical data that you input into the model. Use accurate and up to date data when running the simulations. And if that data is not available, this method will not be suitable for your project. Now let's look at how Burndown charts are used in Agile budgeting. As you know, Burndown charts track the amount of work remaining in the project over time. As the project progresses, the amount of work remaining should decrease at a predictable rate. This allows you to see how much progress is being made and identify any potential problems early on.

By keeping track of your project's burn rate, you will better understand how much money you are spending each month and where you can cut costs if necessary. Finally, here are a few more tips to keep in mind for ensuring the budget stays on track. Number one, understanding the process. Make sure everyone on your team understands the budgeting process. This will help avoid misunderstandings down the line. Number two, keep it realistic. Work with your stakeholders to create a realistic budget that takes into account all of the potential costs associated with your project. Do not make promises you cannot keep or try to cut corners. Number three, Communication.

Always keep communication open with your team and stakeholders about the state of the budget. This will help ensure that everyone is on the same page and that there are no surprises down the road. No project manager wants to reveal that the project has gone over budget, but transparency goes a long way in taking corrective action as early as possible. Diligence and proper planning are the keys to keeping Agile budgets on track. Before we move on to chapter four, download and complete the Agile Budgeting Worksheet. See you in the next chapter.

Overcoming Challenges And Optimising Agile Processes

Welcome to chapter four. Implementing Agile can be fraught with challenges as it requires a different way of thinking about work and a different set of tools and processes. Some of the biggest challenges when it comes to implementing Agile are, number one, lack of attention to the bigger picture. Number two, lack of communication and collaboration. Number three, implementation challenges. Number four, transitioning to Agile. Number five, resistance to change. And number six, scope creep. In this chapter. We'll go through these challenges and explain how to overcome them. Number one, lack of attention to the bigger picture. In Agile, it's important to focus on the big picture and not get bogged down in individual tasks. Failing to do so risks the team losing sight of the value being provided to the customer.

Focusing on the bigger picture can be difficult for companies who are used to working in a more traditional style. Creating user stories can help you to overcome this challenge. Helping everyone involved stay focused on both the specific requirements and the overall goal for the client and end customers. Number two, lack of communication and collaboration. This can happen when team members are not used to working together closely. This may occur when the team members are not used to working with Agile methodology and in newly formed teams where the members are not used to each other's working and communication styles.

To overcome this challenge, it's important to set up regular communication channels such as standups and retrospective meetings and make sure everyone is aware of their roles and responsibilities.

Also make sure that everyone is adequately trained on the Agile process. Ensure that all team members have a shared understanding of the project's goals and objectives, and finally establish clear channels of communication between all members of the team so that information can flow freely and efficiently. With a large proportion of the workforce now working within hybrid and distributed teams, it's important to review your remote communication strategies and ensure they align with the Agile methodology. Make sure each team member is actively using a tool such as Slack so that everyone is on the same page and maintain a regular check in schedule as you would normally if you're working with a distributed team.

Time zones can be a big challenge. It's important to be aware of the different time zones your team members are in and to try to accommodate them as much as possible. There are a few things you can do to make communication easier. Use a time zone converter tool like world time Study.com to help you keep track of what time it is in different regions. Make sure you schedule any calls or meetings at times that are convenient for everyone on the team. Or if that's not always possible, make sure that any mission critical members are there, along with as many other team members as possible. You may have to have some calls during odd hours, but it's worth it to make sure everyone can participate. When team members are living in significantly different time zones, daily standup meetings may not be feasible in this case.

It's important to find an alternative way to set check-ins as often as possible, even if this means sending updates by email to team members that can't attend or summarizing the contents of your meetings on your Slack channel so those members can catch up later. Following these tips, you can make sure that time zone differences don't become a barrier to effective communication. And now let's move on to the next challenge. Number three, implementation challenges. Finally, there are often challenges that come up during the implementation phase of Agile. This can be anything from technical problems to team members not being able to work together effectively as well as factors based on the nature of the work.

To overcome these challenges, make sure you have a detailed plan in place that can be put into action when necessary. Number four Transitioning to Agile. When transitioning to Agile development, it is important to build a sturdy foundation by building a strong team of individuals that are committed to the success of the project. Encourage feedback and collaboration among team members. Feedback is essential in the Agile development process as it allows for continuous improvement. Make sure to create an environment where team members feel comfortable giving and receiving feedback. Another issue that may come up when transitioning to Agile or when onboarding employees that are new to Agile is resistance to change. There are many reasons why teams may resist the Agile methodology.

They may be unfamiliar with the process or they may feel that it's too rigid and does not allow for enough flexibility. Or perhaps they're comfortable with the way things have always been done and are hesitant to change their workflow. Fortunately, there are a few things you can do to overcome resistance and help your team transition to using Agile successfully. Also note that if your team seems resistant to change, it may simply be that they don't understand agile principles as well as you thought. There's always a chance that there are knowledge gaps and graduates are a good example of this. They may have studied Agile and other methodologies but haven't had real world experience with it, so they will not have consolidated their theoretical knowledge through hands-on experience.

Assess whether your team truly understands what it means to use the Agile methodology and if necessary, arrange additional chapters so they can take on board the key principles and better understand the methods of working. Many people resist change because they don't understand how it will benefit them. When explaining the switch to Agile, be sure to highlight all of the ways that it can help improve the team's efficiency and effectiveness and any ways it may benefit them on a personal level. Address any concerns that team members may have. Often people just need their questions and concerns to be heard in order to feel more comfortable with the change. Take the time to truly listen to these concerns and have empathy for their point of view.

Where feasible, make adaptations to accommodate individual needs. In fact, it's good practice to design a method of working that your team can get on board with, whether they have specific concerns or not. Next, create a plan for how the team will transition to using Agile and again, make sure that everyone is on board with the plan. Be patient and flexible as the team adapts to the new methodology and be prepared to answer any questions or address any concerns that may come up. It may take some time to adjust, so don't expect things to be perfect from day one. If your team is feeling frustrated at any point, remind them that there is a learning curve associated with any new system or methodology.

Finally, encourage your team to provide feedback throughout the transition process. This will help you to identify any potential obstacles and make necessary adjustments along the way. Making the switch to Agile can be a challenge, but it's well worth the effort. By taking the time to overcome team resistance, you'll set your team up for success with this powerful methodology. Number six Scope Creep. Agile can be susceptible to scope creep, and this is another reason it's important to have some contingency funds built into the project budget. It is often caused by poorly defined objectives, unrealistic expectations and a lack of communication and is one of the most common causes of project failure.

So keep in mind the following tips to make sure scope creep doesn't creep up on you. It's important that everyone involved has a clear understanding of the project scope from the very beginning. The project scope should be reviewed and approved by all stakeholders before any work begins. And once work starts, any changes to the scope should be carefully planned and tracked. Regular communication between all team members can help keep everyone on the same page and prevent scope creep. Creating detailed user stories and acceptance criteria for each requirement will help ensure that only features that are essential to the success of the project are included and that all features are properly scoped. Also, remember to prioritize features based on business value and do not add new features after the project has started.

This will help ensure that only the most important features are developed and that scope creep does not get out of control. Finally have regular stakeholder meetings to review progress and ensure that scope creep is not happening. This will give everyone involved in the project visibility into what is being delivered and will allow for Book correction if necessary. Scope creep can be a challenge when using Agile, but by following these tips you can keep it under control and deliver a successful project. And with that you've reached the end of chapter four. Your task now is to download and complete the overcoming challenges and optimizing Agile Processes Worksheet. After that, join me in chapter five where we'll be discussing how to boost team engagement and align your Agile processes with individual needs.

Engagement And Individual Needs

Welcome to chapter five. Here, we'll discuss how you can make the most of the Agile methodology to boost team engagement, as well as how to accommodate individual needs and working styles. Many employees find Agile working to be more engaging than traditional work styles. That's because it allows for more autonomy and creativity and it encourages constant learning. Agile provides an opportunity for companies to empower employees, and it gives them more ownership over their work. It also encourages all team members in contributing to important decisions. As we discussed in chapter three, when we looked at determining the confidence level for calculating the contingency budget. But how can you get the most out of Agile in terms of engagement? Here are a few tips.

Number one rewards. Agile provides the perfect framework for incentivizing employees due to the sprint framework. If the team knows that at the end of each sprint, there will be a reward for them, Their motivation will be boosted and they'll be keen to get through the work and cross the finish line. So build some incentives into your process and get your team fired up in line with the Agile spirit. Number two, encourage stewardship. Allow your team to be stewards of the project. Create a culture of stewardship and show them you trust them. This doesn't mean your management style needs to be hands off. And Of course that wouldn't work with Agile anyway.

However, it's about nurturing the sense of ownership that Agile naturally instills in teams. Number three aims to be good enough to maintain engagement. It's important to relieve the pressure of perfectionism. Having a clear definition of done prevents perfectionism and allows employees to feel good about work that is good enough, even if it's not perfect. Moving on, let's discuss how you can make sure you meet the needs of your team members when using the Agile methodology. Doing so is yet another way to ensure all members feel valued and stay engaged. One of the biggest challenges with Agile working is that it can be disruptive to employees schedules and routines.

Many employees are used to working in a more traditional way and they may find the constant meetings and changes to be annoying. In addition, different members of the team may need less support or supervision. Those who are naturally more independent in their working style may feel that constant check-ins are a form of micromanaging. Disruption to routines may especially affect some neurodivergent individuals. Neurodiversity is a term used to describe the range of differences in people's brains and nervous systems. This includes conditions like ADHD, autism and dyslexia. Some people see neurodiversity as a form of diversity similar to racial diversity.

Others see it as a disability rights movement aimed at promoting acceptance and understanding of Neurodivergent people. 15 to 20% of the global population are neurodivergent, but the real number could be significantly greater as some conditions often go unnoticed. For example, it is notoriously common for autism to go undetected in women or be misdiagnosed. Neurodiversity is often seen as a positive thing, as it can lead to different ways of thinking and new perspectives. In fact, research by i.t. Giant Hewlett Packard Enterprise showed that neurodiverse teams are 30% more productive.

And a report by investment company JPMorgan Chase revealed that individuals participating in their autism at work initiative were 90 to 140% more productive than neurotypical employees, and they made fewer errors. Remember, neurodiversity covers a wide range of conditions and individual needs. As such, it is not possible to make generalizations about what will or will not work for all neurodivergent people. In addition, individual needs vary greatly among people with the same diagnosis. With that said, there are some key considerations that can help to inform the decision. There are some key characteristics of agile working that could make it a good fit for neurodivergent individuals.

For example, Agile working practices often involve short focused bursts of activity, which can be less overwhelming than traditional work patterns that require sustained focus over long periods of time. But again, this is not the case for everyone, as this very same principle may frustrate some individuals and make it difficult for them to concentrate. Some individuals with autistic spectrum disorder as well as Attention Deficit Hyperactivity Disorder, or ADHD, may struggle with task switching, while many individuals with ADHD struggle to focus for long periods. Others experience what is known as hyper focus. Hyper focus is characterized by an intense focus on one thing to the exclusion of everything else. This allows the individual to get lost in their work and achieve a high level of productivity.

Once it is triggered, it can be very difficult to break out of the focus and pay attention to other things. Therefore, asking individuals that experience hyper focus to break their concentration for something that is not crucial for them to attend is likely to be very frustrating for them as well as counterproductive as they will then need to re-establish their focus again later. And since it does not always come on in a predictable way, there is no guarantee they will experience that state again, meaning that they have lost the opportunity to achieve great things on that particular occasion. Changing between different types of tasks is known as task switching, and it may be necessary to limit the amount of task switching you ask of Neurodivergent employees as well as individuals with ADHD. Task switching is a common issue for individuals with autism.

Having stand up meetings every day, along with any additional meetings an individual is required to attend can be overwhelming and disrupt some individuals ability to focus throughout the day. Therefore, it may be best to organize meetings for the start or end of the day, leaving them with a large block of time in which they can focus on work. Another area to consider is the social dynamic. Additionally, Agile working often takes place in small teams, which can provide a supportive and understanding environment for neurodivergent individuals. In contrast, traditional work environments can sometimes be more stressful and isolating for those with neurodiverse conditions.

However, some individuals with such conditions may prefer working with limited social contact. Of course, every individual is different and there is no guarantee that Agile working practices will suit everyone with a neurodiverse condition. However, it is worth considering these factors when making a decision about how to implement an Agile approach and which compromises may be necessary to ensure the team performs at their best. Also note that there is a good chance of their being undiagnosed employees who experience the same struggles. So it's important that regardless of whether or not your team involves diagnosed neurodivergent individuals, it's always best practice to consult everyone involved to make sure you can find a mutual agreement with required compromise and necessary accommodations.

Align meetings with the correct windows in which people will naturally have breaks in their flow of work. Limit meetings. Adapt the methodology to have stand up meetings less often than the usual approach to help employees adjust to an agile working style. It's important to be flexible and adaptable, allow employees to work in ways that fit their individual needs and give them the opportunity to provide feedback along the way about how they're getting on with the process and whether any adjustments can be made to improve it. The Agile methodology is not supposed to be a strict set of rules and it can be adapted as required regardless of whether your team includes neurodiverse individuals.

Does your project really require you to have a stand up? Meeting every day or would 2 to 3 times per week be enough? Can you substitute stand up meetings for a thorough project management system that lets you easily see how everyone is getting on at any given moment? Congratulations. You've reached the end of this Book on Agile business processes. Before proceeding to the final chapter where we'll review all the key takeaways, download and complete the Individual Needs and Engagement worksheet where you'll reflect on how you can best support your team members by adapting the Agile methodology.

Conclusion

Once again, congratulations on completing the Book. Let's review the key takeaways we covered throughout the chapters. To start with, we reviewed the benefits of Agile, including rapid response to change, improved communication and cost savings. We then explored the key practices required for making Agile successful. They were having a strong team backbone, delivering value to the customer, embracing change, short interactions, communication and continuously reviewing and improving processes. Next, we recapped all the key concepts in Agile, including the different types of meetings, how projects are structured, the roles within an Agile team, and some terms specific to agile software development. After that we moved on to Agile budgeting.

We reviewed how agile pricing is either based on time and materials or a fixed price quote. We looked at the method for calculating per sprint budgets. You can take the daily rate for each team member and multiply that by the percentage of the time they will be working on the project. For example, for full time workers it would be 100%. You then multiply the result by the number of working days in each sprint for fixed price jobs. You calculate the sprint budget simply by dividing the total price by the number of sprints. We then looked at calculating the contingency budget using the confidence level.

The confidence level is calculated by certain team members voting on a percentage of confidence, then taking an average. The higher the level of confidence, the lower the contingency budget, which is usually between 10 and 50%. We then reviewed how Burndown charts are a good way to keep track of spending. After that, we explored some of the most common challenges that occur in Agile and how to overcome them. We highlighted the importance of focusing on the bigger picture instead of getting bogged down in individual tasks. We also gave tips for ensuring that communication is consistent, such as by ensuring regular check-ins.

This is crucial when team members are not used to working together closely in the way Agile requires. We then reviewed the importance of being prepared for implementation challenges such as technical and interpersonal difficulties. It's crucial to have a plan in place to tackle such challenges to make sure the project stays on track. After that, we explored how to overcome challenges when transitioning to Agile. This included overcoming team resistance to change, highlighting the benefits for the individual, encouraging feedback and being flexible and willing to adapt the process down the line.

Next, we looked at how to prevent scope creep by ensuring thorough planning and creating user stories with clear acceptance criteria to gain clarity about the project scope in the beginning. Maintaining transparency with stakeholders is also vital and you should hold regular meetings with them to review progress. In the final chapter we looked at ways you can increase team engagement using the Agile methodology. This included building and rewards at the end of each sprint, as well as encouraging stewardship and relieving the pressure of perfectionism. We then looked at accommodating individual needs, including the needs of the neurodivergent individuals that make up 15 to 20% of the population.

We discussed the principles of task switching and hyperfocus and why it's so important to minimize disruption in the working day for these individuals, allowing them to focus in the way that they need to. We hope this Book has been enlightening and will enhance the way you approach the Agile methodology in your role. We have a whole catalog Of courses available, so be sure to check out the categories and topics relevant to you and your organization. Best wishes from the Expert Academy and good luck.

Don't miss out!

Visit the website below and you can sign up to receive emails whenever Gaurav Sanjiv Kalangan publishes a new book. There's no charge and no obligation.

https://books2read.com/r/B-A-EPFBB-WRUZC

BOOKS2READ

Connecting independent readers to independent writers.

Also by Gaurav Sanjiv Kalangan

Learn Options Strategies Options Basics & Greeks For Stock Trading By Technical Analysis
Bitcoin, Altcoins & ICOs Learn the Basics of Digital Coins from Zero
Time Management This Is How I Work 300 Percent Faster
How To Build And Implement A Winning Pricing Strategy
Networking For Introverts: Gracefully Exiting A Conversation
Accounting 101: Learn Cost Accounting From A To Z
Growth Marketing: Strategy & Execution Bootcamp For Startups
Develop The Mental Strength Of A Warrior For Success In Life
Time Management Mastery: Productivity & Goals